Fractions, Percents, and Decimals

Name That Portion

Grade 5

Also appropriate for Grade 6

Joan Akers
Cornelia Tierney
Claryce Evans
Megan Murray

LEWIS MIDDLE SCHOOL
5170 Greenbrier Avenue
San Diego CA 92120

Developed at TERC, Cambridge, Massachusetts

Dale Seymour Publications®
White Plains, New York

The *Investigations* curriculum was developed at TERC (formerly Technical Education Research Centers) in collaboration with Kent State University and the State University of New York at Buffalo. The work was supported in part by National Science Foundation Grant No. ESI-9050210. TERC is a nonprofit company working to improve mathematics and science education. TERC is located at 2067 Massachusetts Avenue, Cambridge, MA 02140.

This project was supported, in part,
by the
National Science Foundation
Opinions expressed are those of the authors
and not necessarily those of the Foundation

Managing Editor: Catherine Anderson

Series Editor: Beverly Cory

Revision Team: Laura Marshall Alavosus, Ellen Harding, Patty Green Holubar, Suzanne Knott, Beverly Hersh Lozoff

ESL Consultant: Nancy Sokol Green

Production/Manufacturing Director: Janet Yearian

Production/Manufacturing Manager: Karen Edmonds

Production/Manufacturing Coordinator: Joe Conte

Design Manager: Jeff Kelly

Design: Don Taka

Illustrations: Susan Jaekel, Carl Yoshihara

Cover: Bay Graphics

Composition: Archetype Book Composition

This book is published by Dale Seymour Publications®, an imprint of Addison Wesley Longman, Inc.

Dale Seymour Publications
10 Bank Street
White Plains, NY 10602
Customer Service: 1-800-872-1100

Copyright © 1998 by Dale Seymour Publications®.
All rights reserved. Printed in the United States of America.

Limited reproduction permission: The publisher grants permission to individual teachers who have purchased this book to reproduce the blackline masters as needed for use with their own students. Reproduction for an entire school or school district or for commercial use is prohibited.

Order number DS47045
ISBN 1-57232-798-7
7 8 9 10-ML-02

Printed on Recycled Paper

TERC

Principal Investigator   Susan Jo Russell

Co-Principal Investigator   Cornelia Tierney

Director of Research and Evaluation   Jan Mokros

Curriculum Development

Joan Akers
Michael T. Battista
Mary Berle-Carman
Douglas H. Clements
Karen Economopoulos
Claryce Evans
Marlene Kliman
Cliff Konold
Jan Mokros
Megan Murray
Ricardo Nemirovsky
Tracy Noble
Andee Rubin
Susan Jo Russell
Margie Singer
Cornelia Tierney

Evaluation and Assessment

Mary Berle-Carman
Jan Mokros
Andee Rubin
Tracey Wright

Teacher Support

Kabba Colley
Karen Economopoulos
Anne Goodrow
Nancy Ishihara
Liana Laughlin
Jerrie Moffett
Megan Murray
Margie Singer
Dewi Win
Virginia Woolley
Tracey Wright
Lisa Yaffee

Administration and Production

Irene Baker
Amy Catlin
Amy Taber

Cooperating Classrooms for This Unit

Jo-Ann Pepicelli
Boston Public Schools
Boston, MA
Laraine Morin
Jan Shafer
Cambridge Friends School
Cambridge, MA
Gail Lauinger
Mendocino Unified School District
Mendocino, CA

Technology Development

Douglas H. Clements
Julie Sarama

Video Production

David A. Smith
Judy Storeygard

Consultants and Advisors

Deborah Lowenberg Ball
Marilyn Burns
Mary Johnson
James J. Kaput
Mary M. Lindquist
Leslie P. Steffe
Grayson Wheatley

Graduate Assistants

Richard Aistrope
Kathryn Battista
Caroline Borrow
William Hunt
Kent State University

Jeffrey Barrett
Julie Sarama
Sudha Swaminathan
Elaine Vukelic
State University of New York at Buffalo

Dan Gillette
Irene Hall
Harvard Graduate School of Education

Revisions and Home Materials

Cathy Miles Grant
Marlene Kliman
Margaret McGaffigan
Kim O'Neil
Megan Murray
Andee Rubin
Susan Jo Russell
Lisa Seyferth
Myriam Steinback
Judy Storeygard
Anna Suarez
Cornelia Tierney
Carol Walker
Tracey Wright

CONTENTS

WHERE TO START

The first-time user of *Name That Portion* should read the following:

When you next teach this same unit, you can begin to read more of the background. Each time you present the unit, you will learn more about how your students understand the mathematical ideas.

Investigations in Number, Data, and Space® is a K–5 mathematics curriculum with four major goals:

- to offer students meaningful mathematical problems
- to emphasize depth in mathematical thinking rather than superficial exposure to a series of fragmented topics
- to communicate mathematics content and pedagogy to teachers
- to substantially expand the pool of mathematically literate students

The *Investigations* curriculum embodies a new approach based on years of research about how children learn mathematics. Each grade level consists of a set of separate units, each offering 2–8 weeks of work. These units of study are presented through investigations that involve students in the exploration of major mathematical ideas.

Approaching the mathematics content through investigations helps students develop flexibility and confidence in approaching problems, fluency in using mathematical skills and tools to solve problems, and proficiency in evaluating their solutions. Students also build a repertoire of ways to communicate about their mathematical thinking, while their enjoyment and appreciation of mathematics grows.

The investigations are carefully designed to invite all students into mathematics—girls and boys, members of diverse cultural, ethnic, and language groups, and students with different strengths and interests. Problem contexts often call on students to share experiences from their family, culture, or community. The curriculum eliminates barriers—such as work in isolation from peers, or emphasis on speed and memorization—that exclude some students from participating successfully in mathematics. The following aspects of the curriculum ensure that all students are included in significant mathematics learning:

- Students spend time exploring problems in depth.
- They find more than one solution to many of the problems they work on.

- They invent their own strategies and approaches, rather than rely on memorized procedures.
- They choose from a variety of concrete materials and appropriate technology, including calculators, as a natural part of their everyday mathematical work.
- They express their mathematical thinking through drawing, writing, and talking.
- They work in a variety of groupings—as a whole class, individually, in pairs, and in small groups.
- They move around the classroom as they explore the mathematics in their environment and talk with their peers.

While reading and other language activities are typically given a great deal of time and emphasis in elementary classrooms, mathematics often does not get the time it needs. If students are to experience mathematics in depth, they must have enough time to become engaged in real mathematical problems. We believe that a minimum of 5 hours of mathematics classroom time a week—about an hour a day—is critical at the elementary level. The scope and pacing of the *Investigations* curriculum are based on that belief.

We explain more about the pedagogy and principles that underlie these investigations in Teacher Notes throughout the units. For correlations of the curriculum to the NCTM Standards and further help in using this research-based program for teaching mathematics, see the following books, available from Dale Seymour Publications:

- *Implementing the* Investigations in Number, Data, and Space® *Curriculum*
- *Beyond Arithmetic: Changing Mathematics in the Elementary Classroom* by Jan Mokros, Susan Jo Russell, and Karen Economopoulos

This book is one of the curriculum units for *Investigations in Number, Data, and Space.* In addition to providing part of a complete mathematics curriculum for your students, this unit offers information to support your own professional development. You, the teacher, are the person who will make this curriculum come alive in the classroom; the book for each unit is your main support system.

Although the curriculum does not include student textbooks, reproducible sheets for student work are provided in the unit and are also available as Student Activity Booklets. Students work actively with objects and experiences in their own environment and with a variety of manipulative materials and technology, rather than with a book of instruction and problems. We strongly recommend use of the overhead projector as a way to present problems, to focus group discussion, and to help students share ideas and strategies.

Ultimately, every teacher will use these investigations in ways that make sense for his or her

particular style, the particular group of students, and the constraints and supports of a particular school environment. Each unit offers information and guidance for a wide variety of situations, drawn from our collaborations with many teachers and students over many years. Our goal in this book is to help you, a professional educator, implement this curriculum in a way that will give all your students access to mathematical power.

Investigation Format

The opening two pages of each investigation help you get ready for the work that follows.

What Happens   This gives a synopsis of each session or block of sessions.

Mathematical Emphasis   This lists the most important ideas and processes students will encounter in this investigation.

What to Plan Ahead of Time   These lists alert you to materials to gather, sheets to duplicate, transparencies to make, and anything else you need to do before starting.

INVESTIGATION 2

Models for Fractions

What Happens

Sessions 1 and 2: Fractions on Clocks In this fraction model, students find fractions that represent the rotation of one hand around a clock face. They play a game, Roll Around the Clock, solving fraction addition problems. Finally, they write fraction addition and subtraction problems for classmates to solve.

Session 3: Fraction Strips Students now work with a linear fraction model as they partition paper strips into halves, thirds, fourths, sixths, and, as a challenge, fifths. They use the strips as they look for ways that they can add two fractions together to equal a third fraction.

Sessions 4 and 5: Fraction Tracks Students complete a set of Fraction Tracks, another linear model, showing all fractions between 0 and 1 for halves, thirds, fourths, fifths, sixths, eighths, and tenths. Students look for fraction equivalents and write about patterns they see. They count by fractions across the Fraction Track gameboard, a set of number lines from 0 to 2. Working in groups, students order fractions by size and play the game Capture Fractions.

Session 6: The Fraction Track Game Students play the Fraction Track Game, turning over Fraction Cards to determine their total move. As the students put together different amounts to equal the fraction turned up, they discover how fractions can be broken into parts with unlike denominators.

Sessions 7 and 8: Fraction Games During Choice Time, students play two or three of the fraction games they have already learned: the In-Between Game, Roll Around the Clock, the Fraction Track Game, and Capture Fractions.

Session 9: Problems with Fractions Students solve word problems using fractions and percents and later share their solution strategies.

Mathematical Emphasis

■ representing fractions as rotation around a circle

■ marking strips into fractional parts

■ finding equivalent fractions

■ ordering fractions

■ adding fractions

32 ■ Investigation 2: Models for Fractions

INVESTIGATION 2

What to Plan Ahead of Time

Materials

■ Fraction cubes, in two colors: 2 per pair (Sessions 1–2, 7–8)

■ Chips, buttons, or small counters to use as game pieces: 20 per group of 3–4 students (Sessions 6–8; optional for Sessions 1–2)

■ Overhead projector and pen (Sessions 1–2, 4–6)

■ Chart paper (Sessions 1–5)

■ Pencils (Session 3)

■ Transparent tape, scissors (Sessions 4–5)

■ Ruler: 1 per student (Sessions 4–5)

■ Fraction Cards from Investigation 1: 1 deck per group of 3–4 students (Sessions 4–8)

■ Class charts and Percent Equivalents Strips from Investigation 1 (Sessions 4–5; 7–8)

Other Preparation

■ Duplicate student sheets and teaching resources (located at the end of this unit) in the following quantities. If you have Student Activity Booklets, copy only the items marked with an asterisk.

For Sessions 1–2
Student Sheet 11, Clock Fractions (p. 149): 1 per student

Student Sheet 12, Clock Fractions Addition Problems (p. 150): 1 per student (homework)

Large Clock Face* (p. 158): 1 transparency and several copies

For Session 3
Student Sheet 13, Fraction Strip Subtraction Problems (p. 151): 1 per student (homework)

For Sessions 4–5
Student Sheet 14, How to Play Capture Fractions (p. 152): 1 per student (homework)

Fraction Track Gameboard (p. 159): 1 per student, and a transparency of page 1*

For Session 6
Student Sheet 15, How to Play the Fraction Track Game (p. 153): 1 per student (homework)

Fraction Track Gameboard, page 1 (p. 159): 1 transparency

For Sessions 7–8
Student Sheet 16, More Everyday Uses of Fractions, Decimals, and Percents (p. 154): 1 per student (homework)

For Session 9
Student Sheet 17, Fractions of Pizza (p. 155): 1 per student

Student Sheet 18, Moves on the Fraction Track (p. 157): 1 per student (homework)

■ Before Session 1, prepare your fraction cubes with a sticker on each face. Write these fractions on the cubes:

Cube 1: $\frac{1}{12}$ $\frac{1}{6}$ $\frac{1}{4}$ $\frac{1}{3}$ $\frac{5}{12}$ $\frac{1}{2}$

Cube 2: $\frac{1}{2}$ $\frac{7}{12}$ $\frac{2}{3}$ $\frac{3}{4}$ $\frac{11}{6}$ $\frac{11}{12}$

■ For Session 3, use a paper cutter and paper in five different colors to prepare fraction strips. Make the strips 8½ inches long by about 1 inch wide. Make a set of five strips, one of each color, per student.

■ After Session 5, fill in the missing fractions on your transparency of the Fraction Track Gameboard, page 1, to use as you introduce the game.

■ Because students will take home their own Fraction Track Gameboards, assemble additional gameboards (1 per 3–4 students) for small group use in Sessions 7–8. First fill in a copy of Gameboard, page 1 (p. 159), then make the copies you need.

Investigation 2: Models for Fractions ■ 33

Sessions Within an investigation, the activities are organized by class session, a session being at least a one-hour math class. Sessions are numbered consecutively through an investigation. Often several sessions are grouped together, presenting a block of activities with a single major focus.

When you find a block of sessions presented together—for example, Sessions 1, 2, and 3—read through the entire block first to understand the overall flow and sequence of the activities. Make some preliminary decisions about how you will divide the activities into three sessions for your class, based on what you know about your students. You may need to modify your initial plans as you progress through the activities, and you may want to make notes in the margins of the pages as reminders for the next time you use the unit.

Be sure to read the Session Follow-Up section at the end of the session block to see what homework assignments and extensions are suggested as you make your initial plans.

While you may be used to a curriculum that tells you exactly what each class session should cover, we have found that the teacher is in a better position to make these decisions. Each unit is flexible and may be handled somewhat differently by every teacher. Although we provide guidance for how many sessions a particular group of activities is likely to need, we want you to be active in determining an appropriate pace and the best transition points for your class. It is not unusual for a teacher to spend more or less time than is proposed for the activities.

Ten-Minute Math At the beginning of some sessions, you will find Ten-Minute Math activities. These are designed to be used in tandem with the investigations, but not during the math hour. Rather, we hope you will do them whenever you have a spare 10 minutes—maybe before lunch or recess, or at the end of the day.

Ten-Minute Math offers practice in key concepts, but not always those being covered in the unit. For example, in a unit on using data, Ten-Minute Math might revisit geometric activities done earlier in the year. Complete directions for the suggested activities are included at the end of each unit.

Materials

- Overhead projector (optional)
- Large Clock Face (transparency and extra copies)
- Equivalents chart
- Student Sheet 11 (1 per student)
- Fraction cubes (set of 2 per pair)
- Game chips (optional, 1 per student)
- Chart paper
- Student Sheet 12 (1 per student, homework)

Sessions 1 and 2

Fractions on Clocks

What Happens

In this fraction model, students find fractions that represent the rotation of one hand around a clock face. They play a game, Roll Around the Clock, solving fraction addition problems. Finally, they write fraction addition and subtraction problems for classmates to solve. Their work focuses on:

- representing fractions as rotation around a circle
- adding fractions

Activity

Clock Fractions

Ask students to look at the clock on the wall. If you don't have a round wall clock, show the Large Clock Face transparency on the overhead.

Pretend that the minute hand on this clock is broken. The broken hand always points to 12. The hour hand still moves around to show the time. When the hour hand moves from 12:00 to 1:00, what fraction of the way around has it gone? ($1/12$) Why is it $1/12$?

To encourage students to think of this as a model of rotation rather than area, demonstrate the turn with your hand.

When the hour hand moves from 12:00 to 3:00, what fraction of the way around has it gone?

Some students may call the fraction one-fourth ($1/4$), and others may say three-twelfths ($3/12$). If students suggest more than one fraction, ask them to explain how both describe that turn. Add $3/12$ to the class Equivalents chart, beside $1/4$.

Imagine now that the hour hand is broken and the minute hand moves. When the minute hand moves from the 12 to the 3, how many minutes have gone by? What fraction is that of an hour, or 60 minutes?

Students may say that it is the same as the hour hand moving from 12:00 to 3:00, or $1/4$. Some might suggest that it is also $15/60$. If no one suggests this fraction, try to elicit it:

34 ■ Investigation 2: Models for Fractions

Activities The activities include pair and small-group work, individual tasks, and whole-class discussions. In any case, students are seated together, talking and sharing ideas during all work times. Students most often work cooperatively, although each student may record work individually.

Choice Time In some units, some sessions are structured with activity choices. In these cases, students may work simultaneously on different activities focused on the same mathematical ideas. Students choose which activities they want to do, and they cycle through them.

You will need to decide how to set up and introduce these activities and how to let students make their choices. Some teachers present them as station activities, in different parts of the room. Some list the choices on the board as reminders or have students keep their own lists.

Tips for the Linguistically Diverse Classroom At strategic points in each unit, you will find concrete suggestions for simple modifications of the teaching strategies to encourage the participation of all students. Many of these tips offer alternative ways to elicit critical thinking from students at varying levels of English proficiency, as well as from other students who find it difficult to verbalize their thinking.

The tips are supported by suggestions for specific vocabulary work to help ensure that all students can participate fully in the investigations. The Preview for the Linguistically Diverse Classroom lists important words that are assumed as part of the working vocabulary of the unit. Second-language learners will need to become familiar with these words in order to understand the problems and activities they will be doing. These terms can be incorporated into students' second-language work before or during the unit. Activities that can be used to present the words are found in the appendix, Vocabulary Support for Second-Language Learners. In addition, ideas for making connections to students' languages and cultures, included on the Preview page, help the class explore the unit's concepts from a multicultural perspective.

Session Follow-Up: Homework   In *Investigations,* homework is an extension of classroom work. Sometimes it offers review and practice of work done in class, sometimes preparation for upcoming activities, and sometimes numerical practice that revisits work in earlier units. Homework plays a role both in supporting students' learning and in helping inform families about the ways in which students in this curriculum work with mathematical ideas.

Depending on your school's homework policies and your own judgment, you may want to assign more homework than is suggested in the units. For this purpose you might use the practice pages, included as blackline masters at the end of this unit, to give students additional work with numbers.

For some homework assignments, you will want to adapt the activity to meet the needs of a variety of students in your class: those with special needs, those ready for more challenge, and second-language learners. You might change the numbers in a problem, make the activity more or less complex, or go through a sample activity with

those who need extra help. You can modify any student sheet for either homework or class use. In particular, making numbers in a problem smaller or larger can make the same basic activity appropriate for a wider range of students.

Another issue to consider is how to handle the homework that students bring back to class—how to recognize the work they have done at home without spending too much time on it. Some teachers hold a short group discussion of different approaches to the assignment; others ask students to share and discuss their work with a neighbor; still others post the homework around the room and give students time to tour it briefly. If you want to keep track of homework students bring in, be sure it ends up in a designated place.

Session Follow-Up: Extensions   Sometimes in Session Follow-Up, you will find suggested extension activities. These are opportunities for some or all students to explore a topic in greater depth or in a different context. They are not designed for "fast" students; mathematics is a multifaceted discipline, and different students will want to go further in different investigations. Look for and encourage the sparks of interest and enthusiasm you see in your students, and use the extensions to help them pursue these interests.

Excursions Some of the *Investigations* units include excursions—blocks of activities that could be omitted without harming the integrity of the unit. This is one way of dealing with the great depth and variety of elementary mathematics—much more than a class has time to explore in any one year. Excursions give you the flexibility to make different choices from year to year, doing the excursion in one unit this time, and next year trying another excursion.

Materials

A complete list of the materials needed for teaching this unit follows the unit overview. Some of these materials are available in kits for the *Investigations* curriculum. Individual items can also be purchased from school supply dealers.

Classroom Materials In an active mathematics classroom, certain basic materials should be available at all times: interlocking cubes, pencils, unlined paper, graph paper, calculators, things to count with, and measuring tools. Some activities in this curriculum require scissors and glue sticks or tape. Stick-on notes and large paper are also useful materials throughout.

So that students can independently get what they need at any time, they should know where these materials are kept, how they are stored, and how they are to be returned to the storage area. For example, interlocking cubes are best stored in towers of ten; then, whatever the activity, they should be returned to storage in groups of ten at the end of the hour. You'll find that establishing such routines at the beginning of the year is well worth the time and effort.

Student Sheets and Teaching Resources Student recording sheets and other teaching tools needed for both class and homework are provided as reproducible blackline masters at the end of each unit. We think it's important that students find their own ways of organizing and recording their work. They need to learn how to explain their thinking with both drawings and written words, and how to organize their results so someone else can understand them. For this reason, we deliberately do not provide student sheets for every activity. Regardless of the form in which students do their work, we recommend that they keep their

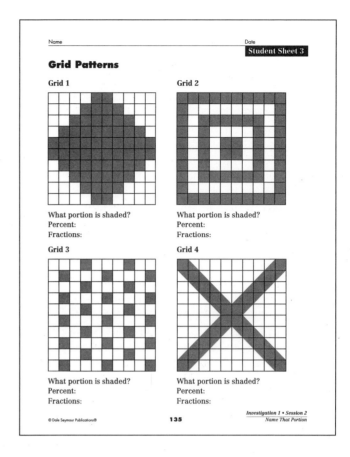

work in a mathematics folder, journal, or notebook so that it is always available to them for reference.

Student Activity Booklets These booklets contain all the sheets each student will need for individual work, freeing you from extensive copying (although you may need or want to copy the occasional teaching resource on transparency film or card stock, or make extra copies of a student sheet).

Calculators and Computers Calculators are used throughout *Investigations*. Many of the units recommend that you have at least one calculator for each pair. You will find calculator activities, plus Teacher Notes discussing this important mathematical tool, in an early unit at each grade level. It is assumed that calculators will be readily available for student use.

Computer activities are offered at all grade levels. How you use the computer activities depends on the number of computers you have available. Technology in the Curriculum discusses ways to incorporate the use of calculators and computers into classroom activities.

Children's Literature Each unit offers a list of related children's literature that can be used to support the mathematical ideas in the unit. Sometimes an activity is based on a specific children's book, with suggestions for substitutions where practical. While such activities can be adapted and taught without the book, the literature offers a rich introduction and should be used whenever possible.

Investigations at Home It is a good idea to make your policy on homework explicit to both students and their families when you begin teaching with *Investigations*. How frequently will you be assigning homework? When do you expect homework to be completed and brought back to school? What are your goals in assigning homework? How independent should families expect their children to be? What should the parent's or guardian's role be? The more explicit you can be about your expectations, the better the homework experience will be for everyone.

Investigations at Home (a booklet available separately for each unit, to send home with students) gives you a way to communicate with families about the work students are doing in class. This booklet includes a brief description of every session, a list of the mathematics content emphasized in each investigation, and a discussion of each homework assignment to help families more effectively support their children. Whether or not you are using the *Investigations* at Home booklets, we expect you to make your own choices about homework assignments. Feel free to omit any and to add extra ones you think are appropriate.

Family Letter A letter that you can send home to students' families is included with the blackline masters for each unit. Families need to be informed about the mathematics work in your classroom; they should be encouraged to participate in and support their children's work. A reminder to send home the letter for each unit appears in one of the early investigations. These letters are also available separately in Spanish, Vietnamese, Cantonese, Hmong, and Cambodian.

Help for You, the Teacher

Because we believe strongly that a new curriculum must help teachers think in new ways about mathematics and about their students' mathematical thinking processes, we have included a great deal of material to help you learn more about both.

About the Mathematics in This Unit This introductory section summarizes the critical information about the mathematics you will be teaching. It describes the unit's central mathematical ideas and the ways students will encounter them through the unit's activities.

About the Assessment in this Unit This introductory section highlights Teacher Checkpoints and assessment activities contained in the unit. It offers questions to stimulate your assessment as you observe the development of students' mathematical thinking and learning.

Teacher Notes These reference notes provide practical information about the mathematics you are teaching and about our experience with how students learn. Many of the notes were written in response to actual questions from teachers or to discuss important things we saw happening in the

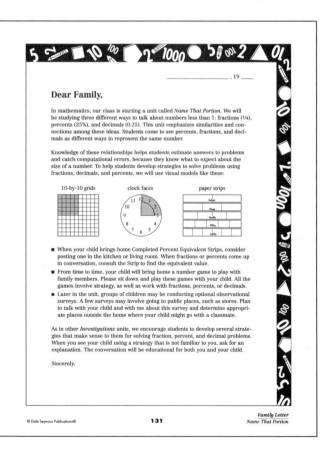

field-test classrooms. Some teachers like to read them all before starting the unit, then review them as they come up in particular investigations.

Dialogue Boxes   Sample dialogues demonstrate how students typically express their mathematical ideas, what issues and confusions arise in their thinking, and how some teachers have guided class discussions.

These dialogues are based on the extensive classroom testing of this curriculum; many are word-for-word transcriptions of recorded class discussions. They are not always easy reading; sometimes it may take some effort to unravel what the students are trying to say. But this is the value of these dialogues; they offer good clues to how your students may develop and express their approaches and strategies, helping you prepare for your own class discussions.

Where to Start   You may not have time to read everything the first time you use this unit. As a first-time user, you will likely focus on understanding the activities and working them out with your students. Read completely through all the activities before starting to present them. Also read those sections listed in the Contents under the heading Where to Start.

Teacher Note ▷   *Decimal Equivalents of Fractions*

Since all fractions are one way to represent the division of two numbers, using calculators makes finding decimal equivalents of fractions very easy. However, it is important that your students develop some understanding of what the results indicate. When the denominator of a fraction is a factor of the numerator, as in $25/5$, the decimal equivalent is a whole number. In all other cases, there will be at least one number following the decimal point.

As your students use calculators to find decimal equivalents of fractions, they will notice that decimal equivalents for these fractions fall into two main groups—decimals that terminate, or end after a certain number of digits, and decimals that fill the calculator display and seem to go on beyond the digits on the display.

All nonterminating decimal equivalents of fractions are called repeating decimals—some or all of the decimal digits repeat. For $5/6$ or $0.8\overline{3}$ (0.833333...), only the 3 repeats. For $2/11$ or $0.\overline{18}$ (0.181818...), two digits repeat. For some fractions, such as $1/3$ (0.$\overline{3}$) or $1/6$ (.1$\overline{6}$), the repeating pattern is quite obvious; for others, such as $1/7$ (0.$\overline{142857}$), it is not. Identifying the repeating pattern is not necessarily easy. For example, $47/49$ begins 0.9591 and goes on for 42 decimal places before it repeats all 42 digits. There is no way of knowing this from an eight-digit calculator display.

For some nonterminating decimals, there is no repeating pattern; these are irrational numbers (numbers that cannot be expressed as the division of two whole numbers). Pi (π) and the square root of 2 are examples of irrational numbers.

In this unit, avoid emphasizing that all fractions will be either terminating or repeating decimals. At this age, your students will have no way of proving why this is true, and there is a danger they will decide that things that appear to be true for a certain number of cases can be generalized as a "proof" for all cases. For example, for repeating decimals, students may assume—incorrectly—that the reappearance of a single digit in a decimal indicates the start of a repeating pattern. This is true for single-digit denominators; for $1/7$, most calculators display 0.1428571, and the second 1 is the beginning of the repeating pattern. But the rule doesn't always work for denominators with more than one digit; $47/49$ obviously has many digits occurring more than once in the 42 digits of its repeating pattern.

D I A L O G U E   B O X

Ordering Decimals

Students are often confused about which zeros in decimals change their value. The teacher in this class walked around as students discussed the difference between 0.5, 0.05, and 0.50. At one table, the teacher heard the following reasoning.

Shakita: I don't see the difference between 0.5, 0.05, and 0.50.

Tai: They're all half of something, aren't they?

Cara: Let's write them as fractions. The first one is tenths, and the other two are both hundredths. I don't remember which zero we can leave off. *[She writes the three as fractions.]*

$$\frac{5}{10} \quad \frac{05}{100} \quad \frac{50}{100}$$

Antonio: It's like the remote on the TV. You can punch in zero five for channel five.

Cara: Then $05/100$ is the same as $5/100$.

Tai: And 0.5 and 0.50 are both halves—5 out of 10, and 50 out of 100.

Shakita: There's no card in the deck that has 0.50 on it.

Tai: Because it's equal to 0.5—remember, there are no cards that are equal in the deck.

Shakita: So 0.05 is a lot smaller than 0.5 because 5 hundredths is much less than 50 hundredths.

The *Investigations* curriculum incorporates the use of two forms of technology in the classroom: calculators and computers. Calculators are assumed to be standard classroom materials, available for student use in any unit. Computers are explicitly linked to one or more units at each grade level; they are used with the unit on 2-D geometry at each grade, as well as with some of the units on measuring, data, and changes.

Using Calculators

In this curriculum, calculators are considered tools for doing mathematics, similar to pattern blocks or interlocking cubes. Just as with other tools, students must learn both *how* to use calculators correctly and *when* they are appropriate to use. This knowledge is crucial for daily life, as calculators are now a standard way of handling numerical operations, both at work and at home.

Using a calculator correctly is not a simple task; it depends on a good knowledge of the four operations and of the number system, so that students can select suitable calculations and also determine what a reasonable result would be. These skills are the basis of any work with numbers, whether or not a calculator is involved.

Unfortunately, calculators are often seen as tools to check computations with, as if other methods are somehow more fallible. Students need to understand that any computational method can be used to check any other; it's just as easy to make a mistake on the calculator as it is to make a mistake on paper or with mental arithmetic. Throughout this curriculum, we encourage students to solve computation problems in more than one way in order to double-check their accuracy. We present mental arithmetic, paper-and-pencil computation, and calculators as three possible approaches.

In this curriculum we also recognize that, despite their importance, calculators are not always appropriate in mathematics instruction. Like any tools, calculators are useful for some tasks but not for others. You will need to make decisions about when to allow students access to calculators and when to ask that they solve problems without them so that they can concentrate on other tools

and skills. At times when calculators are or are not appropriate for a particular activity, we make specific recommendations. Help your students develop their own sense of which problems they can tackle with their own reasoning and which ones might be better solved with a combination of their own reasoning and the calculator.

Managing calculators in your classroom so that they are a tool, and not a distraction, requires some planning. When calculators are first introduced, students often want to use them for everything, even problems that can be solved quite simply by other methods. However, once the novelty wears off, students are just as interested in developing their own strategies, especially when these strategies are emphasized and valued in the classroom. Over time, students will come to recognize the ease and value of solving problems mentally, with paper and pencil, or with manipulatives, while also understanding the power of the calculator to facilitate work with larger numbers.

Experience shows that if calculators are available only occasionally, students become excited and distracted when they are permitted to use them. They focus on the tool rather than on the mathematics. In order to learn when calculators are appropriate and when they are not, students must have easy access to them and use them routinely in their work.

If you have a calculator for each student, and if you think your students can accept the responsibility, you might allow them to keep their calculators with the rest of their individual materials, at least for the first few weeks of school. Alternatively, you might store them in boxes on a shelf, number each calculator, and assign a corresponding number to each student. This system can give students a sense of ownership while also helping you keep track of the calculators.

Using Computers

Students can use computers to approach and visualize mathematical situations in new ways. The computer allows students to construct and manipulate geometric shapes, see objects move according to rules they specify, and turn, flip, and repeat a pattern.

This curriculum calls for computers in units where they are a particularly effective tool for learning mathematics content. One unit on 2-D geometry at each of the grades 3–5 includes a core of activities that rely on access to computers, either in the classroom or in a lab. Other units on geometry, measuring, data, and changes include computer activities, but can be taught without them. In these units, however, students' experience is greatly enhanced by computer use.

The following list outlines the recommended use of computers in this curriculum:

Kindergarten
Unit: *Making Shapes and Building Blocks*
  (Exploring Geometry)
Software: *Shapes*
Source: provided with the unit

Grade 1
Unit: *Survey Questions and Secret Rules*
  (Collecting and Sorting Data)
Software: *Tabletop, Jr.*
Source: Broderbund

Unit: *Quilt Squares and Block Towns*
  (2-D and 3-D Geometry)
Software: *Shapes*
Source: provided with the unit

Grade 2
Unit: *Mathematical Thinking at Grade 2*
  (Introduction)
Software: *Shapes*
Source: provided with the unit

Unit: *Shapes, Halves, and Symmetry*
  (Geometry and Fractions)
Software: *Shapes*
Source: provided with the unit

Unit: *How Long? How Far?* (Measuring)
Software: *Geo-Logo*
Source: provided with the unit

Grade 3
Unit: *Flips, Turns, and Area* (2-D Geometry)
Software: *Tumbling Tetrominoes*
Source: provided with the unit

Unit: *Turtle Paths* (2-D Geometry)
Software: *Geo-Logo*
Source: provided with the unit

Grade 4
Unit: *Sunken Ships and Grid Patterns*
  (2-D Geometry)
Software: *Geo-Logo*
Source: provided with the unit

Grade 5
Unit: *Picturing Polygons* (2-D Geometry)
Software: *Geo-Logo*
Source: provided with the unit

Unit: *Patterns of Change* (Tables and Graphs)
Software: *Trips*
Source: provided with the unit

Unit: *Data: Kids, Cats, and Ads* (Statistics)
Software: *Tabletop, Sr.*
Source: Broderbund

The software provided with the *Investigations* units uses the power of the computer to help students explore mathematical ideas and relationships that cannot be explored in the same way with physical materials. With the *Shapes* (grades 1–2) and *Tumbling Tetrominoes* (grade 3) software, students explore symmetry, pattern, rotation and reflection, area, and characteristics of 2-D shapes. With the *Geo-Logo* software (grades 2–5), students investigate rotations and reflections, coordinate geometry, the properties of 2-D shapes, and angles. The *Trips* software (grade 5) is a mathematical exploration of motion in which students run experiments and interpret data presented in graphs and tables.

We suggest that students work in pairs on the computer; this not only maximizes computer resources but also encourages students to consult, monitor, and teach each other. Generally, more than two students at one computer find it difficult to share. Managing access to computers is an issue for every classroom. The curriculum gives you explicit support for setting up a system. The units are structured on the assumption that you have enough computers for half your students to work on the machines in pairs at one time. If you do not have access to that many computers, suggestions are made for structuring class time to use the unit with fewer than five.

Assessment plays a critical role in teaching and learning, and it is an integral part of the *Investigations* curriculum. For a teacher using these units, assessment is an ongoing process. You observe students' discussions and explanations of their strategies on a daily basis and examine their work as it evolves. While students are busy recording and representing their work, working on projects, sharing with partners, and playing mathematical games, you have many opportunities to observe their mathematical thinking. What you learn through observation guides your decisions about how to proceed. In any of the units, you will repeatedly consider questions like these:

- Do students come up with their own strategies for solving problems, or do they expect others to tell them what to do? What do their strategies reveal about their mathematical understanding?

- Do students understand that there are different strategies for solving problems? Do they articulate their strategies and try to understand other students' strategies?

- How effectively do students use materials as tools to help with their mathematical work?

- Do students have effective ideas for keeping track of and recording their work? Do keeping track of and recording their work seem difficult for them?

You will need to develop a comfortable and efficient system for recording and keeping track of your observations. Some teachers keep a clipboard handy and jot notes on a class list or on adhesive labels that are later transferred to student files. Others keep loose-leaf notebooks with a page for each student and make weekly notes about what they have observed in class.

Assessment Tools in the Unit

With the activities in each unit, you will find questions to guide your thinking while observing the students at work. You will also find two built-in assessment tools: Teacher Checkpoints and embedded Assessment activities.

Teacher Checkpoints   The designated Teacher Checkpoints in each unit offer a time to "check in" with individual students, watch them at work, and ask questions that illuminate how they are thinking.

At first it may be hard to know what to look for, hard to know what kinds of questions to ask. Students may be reluctant to talk; they may not be accustomed to having the teacher ask them about their work, or they may not know how to explain their thinking. Two important ingredients of this process are asking students open-ended questions about their work and showing genuine interest in how they are approaching the task. When students see that you are interested in their thinking and are counting on them to come up with their own ways of solving problems, they may surprise you with the depth of their understanding.

Teacher Checkpoints also give you the chance to pause in the teaching sequence and reflect on how your class is doing overall. Think about whether you need to adjust your pacing: Are most students fluent with strategies for solving a particular kind of problem? Are they just starting to formulate good strategies? Or are they still struggling with how to start? Depending on what you see as the students work, you may want to spend more time on similar problems, change some of the problems to use smaller numbers, move quickly to more-challenging material, modify subsequent activities for some students, work on particular ideas with a small group, or pair students who have good strategies with those who are having more difficulty.

Embedded Assessment Activities   Assessment activities embedded in each unit will help you examine specific pieces of student work, figure out what they mean, and provide feedback. From the students' point of view, these assessment activities are no different from any others. Each is a learning experience in and of itself, as well as an opportunity for you to gather evidence about students' mathematical understanding.

The embedded assessment activities sometimes involve writing and reflecting; at other times, a discussion or brief interaction between student and teacher; and in still other instances, the creation and explanation of a product. In most cases, the assessments require that students *show* what they did, *write* or *talk* about it, or do both. Having to explain how they worked through a problem helps students be more focused and clear in their mathematical thinking. It also helps them realize that doing mathematics is a process that may involve tentative starts, revising one's approach, taking different paths, and working through ideas.

Teachers often find the hardest part of assessment to be interpreting their students' work. We provide guidelines to help with that interpretation. If you have used a process approach to teaching writing, the assessment in *Investigations* will seem familiar. For many of the assessment activities, a Teacher Note provides examples of student work and a commentary on what it indicates about student thinking.

Documentation of Student Growth

To form an overall picture of mathematical progress, it is important to document each student's work. Many teachers have students keep their work in folders, notebooks, or journals, and some like to have students summarize their learning in journals at the end of each unit. It's important to document students' progress, and we recommend that you keep a portfolio of selected work for each student, unit by unit, for the entire year. The final activity in each *Investigations* unit, called Choosing Student Work to Save, helps you and the students select representative samples for a record of their work.

This kind of regular documentation helps you synthesize information about each student as a mathematical learner. From different pieces of evidence, you can put together the big picture. This synthesis will be invaluable in thinking about where to go next with a particular child, deciding where more work is needed, or explaining to parents (or other teachers) how a child is doing.

If you use portfolios, you need to collect a good balance of work, yet avoid being swamped with an overwhelming amount of paper. Following are some tips for effective portfolios:

- Collect a representative sample of work, including some pieces that students themselves select for inclusion in the portfolio. There should be just a few pieces for each unit, showing different kinds of work—some assignments that involve writing as well as some that do not.

- If students do not date their work, do so yourself so that you can reconstruct the order in which pieces were done.

- Include your reflections on the work. When you are looking back over the whole year, such comments are reminders of what seemed especially interesting about a particular piece; they can also be helpful to other teachers and to parents. Older students should be encouraged to write their own reflections about their work.

Assessment Overview

There are two places to turn for a preview of the assessment opportunities in each *Investigations* unit. The Assessment Resources column in the unit Overview Chart identifies the Teacher Checkpoints and Assessment activities embedded in each investigation, guidelines for observing the students that appear within classroom activities, and any Teacher Notes and Dialogue Boxes that explain what to look for and what types of student responses you might expect to see in your classroom. Additionally, the section About the Assessment in This Unit gives you a detailed list of questions for each investigation, keyed to the mathematical emphases, to help you observe student growth.

Depending on your situation, you may want to provide additional assessment opportunities. Most of the investigations lend themselves to more frequent assessment, simply by having students do more writing and recording while they are working.

Name That Portion

Content of This Unit Students use a variety of models, including grids, number lines, and clock faces, as they find fraction, percent, and decimal equivalencies and solve computation problems that involve amounts less than 1. In a survey project, they collect data about two groups and represent the data using fractions and percents, which they then show in circle graphs.

Connections with Other Units If you are doing the full-year *Investigations* curriculum in the suggested sequence for grade 5, this is the third of nine units. It builds on an understanding of fractions as presented in two grade 4 units, *Different Shapes, Equal Pieces* (Fractions and Area) and *Three out of Four Like Spaghetti* (Data and Fractions). Another grade 4 unit, *Money, Miles, and Large Numbers,* deals with decimals in the context of money and odometer readings.

The understanding of fractions and percents that is developed in *Name That Portion* gets practical use when students compare data sets in the grade 5 Statistics unit, *Data: Kids, Cat, and Ads.*

This unit can also be used successfully at grade 6, depending on the previous experience and needs of your students.

Investigations Curriculum ■ Suggested Grade 5 Sequence

Mathematical Thinking at Grade 5 (Introduction and Landmarks in the Number System)

Picturing Polygons (2-D Geometry)

▶ *Name That Portion* (Fractions, Percents, and Decimals)

Between Never and Always (Probability)

Building on Numbers You Know (Computation and Estimation Strategies)

Measurement Benchmarks (Estimating and Measuring)

Patterns of Change (Tables and Graphs)

Containers and Cubes (3-D Geometry: Volume)

Data: Kids, Cats, and Ads (Statistics)

Investigation 1 ■ Exploring Percents and Fractions

Class Sessions	Activities	Pacing
Session 1 (p. 4) CONNECTING FRACTIONS, DECIMALS, AND PERCENTS	Fractions, Decimals, and Percents Teacher Checkpoint: Showing What You Know Homework: Everyday Uses of Fractions, Decimals, and Percents Extension: Fractions, Decimals, and Percents Collage	minimum 1 hr
Session 2 (p. 10) PERCENT GRID PATTERNS	What Fraction Do You See? Interpreting Percents Grid Patterns as Percents Making Grid Patterns Homework: What Fraction Do You See? Extension: More Everyday Uses of Fractions, Decimals, and Percents Extension: Percent and Fraction Patterns Extension: Fraction/Percent/Decimal Display Extension: Using the Grid Patterns	minimum 1 hr
Sessions 3 and 4 (p. 18) FRACTION AND PERCENT GRIDS	Fourths and Eighths on Grids Finding Fraction and Percent Equivalents Discussion: Equivalent Fractions and Percents Homework: Seeing Fractions and Percents on Grids Homework: Grouping Equivalent Fractions	minimum 2 hr
Sessions 5 and 6 (p. 24) PERCENT EQUIVALENTS STRIPS	Teacher Checkpoint: Marking a Percent Equivalents Strip Playing the In-Between Game Homework: The In-Between Game	minimum 2 hr
Session 7 (p. 29) FRACTION AND PERCENT PROBLEMS	Assessment: Fraction and Percent Problems Homework: 2/3 and 3/4	minimum 1 hr

Ten-Minute Math ■ Seeing Numbers

Mathematical Emphasis

- Using fractions to describe how many in a group share a particular characteristic

- Finding equivalent fractions and percents

- Representing, identifying, and ordering fractions and percents; using 1/2 and 1 as references

- Interpreting common uses of percent

- Building on knowledge of unit fractions to use fractions with numerators greater than 1

Assessment Resources

Teacher Checkpoint: Showing What You Know (p. 6)

About Teaching Fractions, Percents, and Decimals Together (Teacher Note, p. 8)

Finding Thirds and Sixths on the Grids (Dialogue Box, p. 23)

Teacher Checkpoint: Marking a Percent Equivalents Strip (p. 24)

Playing the In-Between Game: Observing the Students (p. 27)

Assessment: Fraction and Percent Problems (p. 29)

Materials

Calculators

Chart paper

Colored pencils, crayons, or markers

Scissors

Envelopes or resealable plastic bags

Overhead projector and pens

Family letter

Student Sheets 1–10

Teaching resource sheets

Investigation 2 ■ Models for Fractions

Class Sessions	Activities	Pacing
Sessions 1 and 2 (p. 34) FRACTIONS ON CLOCKS	Clock Fractions Adding Fractions on the Clock Roll Around the Clock Game Writing Fraction Problems Homework: Clock Fractions Addition Problems	minimum 2 hr
Session 3 (p. 41) FRACTION STRIPS	Teacher Checkpoint: Marking Fraction Strips Using the Strips for Fraction Sums Homework: Fraction Strip Subtraction Problems	minimum 1 hr
Sessions 4 and 5 (p. 46) FRACTION TRACKS	Halfway Across the Fraction Tracks Labeling the Fraction Tracks Patterns on the Fraction Tracks Counting by Fractions Ordering the Fraction Cards Capture Fractions Game Homework: More In-Between Homework: Capture Fractions Extension: Number Lines in Use	minimum 2 hr
Session 6 (p. 53) THE FRACTION TRACK GAME	Introducing the Fraction Track Game Playing the Fraction Track Game Homework: The Fraction Track Game	minimum 1 hr
Sessions 7 and 8 (p. 58) FRACTION GAMES	Choice Time: Fraction Games Homework: More Everyday Uses of Fractions, Decimals, and Percents Extension: Making Moves on Two and Three Tracks	minimum 2 hr
Session 9 (p. 62) PROBLEMS WITH FRACTIONS	Fractions of Pizza Homework: Moves on the Fraction Track	minimum 1 hr

◔ **Ten-Minute Math** ■ **Seeing Numbers**

Mathematical Emphasis	Assessment Resources	Materials
■ Representing fractions as rotation around a circle ■ Marking strips into fractional parts ■ Finding equivalent fractions ■ Ordering fractions ■ Adding fractions	Roll Around the Clock Game: Observing the Students (p. 39) Teacher Checkpoint: Marking Fraction Strips (p. 42) Students' Strategies for Partitioning Strips (Teacher Note, p. 45) Equivalents on the Fraction Tracks (Dialogue Box, p. 52) Playing the Fraction Track Game (Dialogue Box, p. 57) Choice Time: Fraction Games: Observing the Students (p. 60) Fractions of Pizza: Observing the Students (p. 62)	Fraction cubes Chips, buttons, or small counters Overhead projector and pen Chart paper Transparent tape Pencils Scissors Ruler Fraction Cards (from Investigation 1) Class charts and Percent Equivalents Strips (from Investigation 1) Student Sheets 11–18 Teaching resource sheets

Investigation 3 ▪ Exploring Decimals

Class Sessions	Activities	Pacing
Session 1 (p. 66) INTERPRETING DECIMALS	Interpreting Decimals Fractions to Decimals on the Calculator Win/Loss Records Extension: Weekly Rainfall Extension: Percentage of Fats in Foods	minimum 1 hr
Session 2 (p. 72) DECIMALS ON GRIDS	Decimals on Grids Fill Two Homework: Fill Two	minimum 1 hr
Sessions 3 and 4 (p. 78) DECIMAL GAMES	Smaller to Larger Game Choice Time: Decimal Games Teacher Checkpoint: Observing Decimal Games Homework: Decimal Games	minimum 2 hr
Sessions 5 and 6 (p. 83) FRACTIONS TO DECIMALS	Comparing Decimals Making a Division Table Patterns in the Division Table Homework: Fraction, Decimal, Percent Equivalents Extension: Guess My Fraction Extension: Fraction Calculators	minimum 2 hr
Session 7 (p. 92) FRACTION, PERCENT, AND DECIMAL PROBLEMS	Scoring Sports and Other Problems Team Rankings Homework: Comparing Common Fractions Extension: Fraction, Percent, and Decimal Equivalents	minimum 1 hr
Session 8 (p. 95) COMPARING FRACTIONAL AMOUNTS	Assessment: Showing Which Is Larger Homework: More Fraction Comparisons Extension: Showing Fraction Addition and Subtraction	minimum 1 hr

◕ **Ten-Minute Math** ▪ **Exploring Data**

Mathematical Emphasis

- Representing and adding decimals on grids

- Reading and writing decimals

- Ordering decimals

- Dividing to find decimal equivalents of fractions

- Comparing fractions using different models and notations

- Making sense of and solving word problems

Assessment Resources

Ordering Decimals (Dialogue Box, p. 77)

Teacher Checkpoint: Observing Decimal Games (p. 81)

Making a Division Table: Observing the Students (p. 86)

Decimal Equivalents of Fractions (Teacher Note, p. 90)

How Much Is Nine Halves? (Dialogue Box, p. 91)

Scoring Sports and Other Problems: Observing the Students (p. 93)

Assessment: Showing Which Is Larger (p. 95)

Materials

Class list, Everyday Uses of Decimals

Newspaper sports section

Calculators

Crayons or colored markers

Overhead projector, pens, blank transparency

Large poster paper

Paper clips or rubber bands

Envelopes or resealable plastic bags

Student Sheets 19–25

Teaching resource sheets

Investigation 4 ■ Data and Percents in Circle Graphs (Excursion)*

Class Sessions	Activities	Pacing
Session 1 (p. 102) PLANNING AGE OR GENDER SURVEYS	Age and Gender Distributions Making Age or Gender Hypotheses Making Survey Plans Homework: Surveys	minimum 1 hr
Session 2 (p. 111) CIRCLE GRAPHS	Making Circle Graphs Using Circle Graphs to Represent Data Homework: Continued Work	minimum 1 hr
Sessions 3 and 4 (p. 114) INTERPRETING PERCENTS	Choice Time: Interpreting Percents Discussing the Choices Homework: More Survey Work	minimum 2 hr
Sessions 5 and 6 (p. 118) SURVEY REPORTS	Preparing Final Reports Sharing the Reports Assessment: Evaluating the Final Reports	minimum 2 hr
Session 7 (p. 121) TWO DAYS IN MY LIFE	A Typical Day Choosing Student Work to Save	minimum 1 hr

* Excursions can be omitted without harming the integrity or continuity of the unit, but offer good mathematical work if you have time to include them.

Mathematical Emphasis

- Planning and conducting surveys

- Organizing and representing data as fractions, percents, and in circle graphs

- Interpreting common uses of fractions, decimals, and percents

Assessment Resources

Making Survey Plans: Observing the Students (p. 107)

Dealing with Gender Issues (Teacher Note, p. 108)

Planning the Surveys (Teacher Note, p. 109)

Possible or Impossible? (Teacher Note, p. 117)

Assessment: Evaluating the Final Reports (p. 119)

A Typical Day: Observing the Students (p. 123)

Choosing Student Work to Save (p. 123)

Materials

Scissors

Overhead projector

Large paper

Crayons or markers

Glue

Large stick-on notes

Student Sheets 26–30

Teaching resource sheets

Following are the basic materials needed for the activities in this unit. Many of the items can be purchased from the publisher, either individually or in the Teacher Resource Package and the Student Materials Kit for grade 5. Detailed information is available on the *Investigations* order form. To obtain this form, call toll-free 1-800-872-1100 and ask for a Dale Seymour customer service representative.

Fraction cubes: Use number cubes or wooden blocks with stickers, on which you write the fractions, covering each face. If possible, the cubes should be two different colors. (Blank cubes and gummed dots for labels are provided in the grade 5 kit.)

Chips or other small objects to use as game pieces: 20 per group of 3–4 students

Ruler or cardboard strip to use as a straightedge: 1 per student

Calculators (available)

Large stick-on notes (at least 3 by 3 inches) or index cards and paper clips: several per student

Envelopes or resealable plastic bags for storing cards: at least 1 per student

Paper clips or rubber bands

Assorted colored pencils, crayons, or marking pens to share: at least 2 colors per student

Chart paper

Large paper (about 11 by 17 inches) or colored paper for making reports and posters: 2 per group

Scissors (1 per student)

Tape (to share)

Pencils

Overhead projector

Overhead transparency markers in two colors

Sports section of a newspaper

Glue

The following materials are provided at the end of this unit as blackline masters. A Student Activity Booklet containing all student sheets and teaching resources needed for individual work is available.

Family Letter (p. 131)

Student Sheets 1–30 (p. 132)

Teaching Resources:

    Percent Equivalents Strips (p. 144)

    Completed Percent Equivalents Strips (p. 145)

    Fraction Cards (p. 146)

    Large Clock Face (p. 158)

    Fraction Track Gameboard (p. 159)

    Decimal Grids (p. 168)

    Decimal Cards, Sets A and B (p. 169)

    Circle Graphs (p. 176)

    Percentractors (p. 177)

    Grids (p. 178)

Practice Pages (p. 179)

Related Children's Literature

Dennis, J. Richard. *Fractions Are Parts of Things.* New York: Thomas Y. Crowell, 1971.

Ernst, Lisa Campbell. *Sam Johnson and the Blue Ribbon Quilt.* New York: Lothrop, Lee and Shepard, 1983.

Fractions, percents, and decimals have traditionally been taught as separate topics, each with its own rules and procedures for calculation. This unit instead emphasizes similarities and connections between these ideas. Students come to see percents, fractions, and decimals as different ways to represent the same number. They develop strategies for finding equivalent notations so that they are able to move back and forth freely among notations and to choose the one most appropriate for a specific situation.

Students focus on relationships among numbers across and within notational systems. For example, they figure out that $1/5$ is equal to 20% because $1/5$ of 100 is 20. Then they build on this to find that $2/5 = 40\%$, $3/5 = 60\%$, and so on. They identify numbers such as $1/2$ and 1 as landmarks, useful as references in judging the size of other numbers.

Fractions and percents are part of our spoken language. We rarely use decimals when we speak, and when we do, we often say them as if they were whole numbers (twenty cents; a batting average of two eighty). However, decimals are easier to compute with than fractions, and they are the language of standard calculators. With increased use of calculators in elementary schools, educators are suggesting that we reduce the emphasis on fractions and teach about computing with decimals earlier.

Even so, this unit does not concentrate on *procedures* for either decimal or fraction computation. Students solve computation problems using good number sense, based on their understanding of the quantities and their relationships. They carry out addition and subtraction of fractional amounts in their own ways and in more than one way, using fractions, decimals, or percents, and using any models that make sense to them. They play games in which they compare and order fractions and decimals, find numbers that fall between two given numbers, and break down fractions into parts of unlike denominators.

Students support their reasoning with a variety of visual models, including rectangular grids, rotations of the hands of a clock, and number lines.

You may find that different models work for different students. In translating between models and between notations, students enrich their understanding of fraction relationships.

Whether written as fractions, decimals, or percents, numbers less than 1 have a complexity of meanings. In order to make sense of and use fractions, students must consider relationships—either between parts and wholes or between different quantities. When students see $3/4$, they must think about the role of the 3 and 4 separately, about how the two numbers are related—that the numerator is $3/4$ of the denominator—and about relationships between $3/4$ and other numbers. The context of the problem helps the students to determine which of the many meanings of $3/4$ is appropriate.

In earlier grades, the *Investigations* curriculum explored both fractions of *area* and fractions of *quantities*. In this unit, as students investigate the proportion of two groups found in certain places or doing certain activities, they deal with fractions as ratios and as parts of a group:

- "In the supermarket, 3 out of 4 people are female." This is a ratio that is independent of the number of people in the market.
- "About $3/4$ of the 100 people I counted, or 75 people, are female." Here the fraction is used as an operation: Divide the number of people who are female by the number who were counted to get the fraction, or multiply the 100 people by the fraction to find the number of females.

At the beginning of each investigation, the Mathematical Emphasis section tells you what is most important for students to learn about during that investigation. Many of these understandings and processes are difficult and complex. Students gradually learn more and more about each idea over many years of schooling. Individual students will begin and end the unit with different levels of knowledge and skill, but all will be better able to interpret fractions, percents, and decimals as quantities and to translate from one notation to another for expressing fractional amounts.

Throughout the *Investigations* curriculum, there are many opportunities for ongoing daily assessment as you observe, listen to, and interact with students at work. In this unit, you will find four Teacher Checkpoints:

Investigation 1, Session 1:
Showing What You Know (p. 6)

Investigation 1, Sessions 5–6:
Marking a Percent Equivalents Strip (p. 24)

Investigation 2, Session 3:
Marking Fraction Strips (p. 42)

Investigation 3, Sessions 3–4:
Observing Decimal Games (p. 81)

This unit also has two embedded assessment activities:

Investigation 1, Session 7:
Fraction and Percent Problems (p. 29)

Investigation 3, Session 8:
Showing Which Is Larger (p. 95)

In addition, you can use almost any activity in this unit to assess your students' needs and strengths. Listed below are questions to help you focus your observation in each investigation. You may want to keep track of your observations for each student to help you plan your curriculum and monitor students' growth. Suggestions for documenting student growth can be found in the section About Assessment.

Investigation 1: Exploring Percents and Fractions

- How do students describe a portion of a group that shares a characteristic? Do they use fractions? percents? (For example, 2 out of 5 is $2/5$ or 40%.)

- How do students find fraction and percent equivalents (for example $1/2$, $3/6$, 50%, and 1 out of 2)?

- What strategies do students use to represent fractions and percents on grids? on number lines? What strategies do they use to order fractions and percents? Do they use $1/2$ and 1 as landmarks, or references? (For example, do they use equivalents?)

- How do students interpret and make sense of common uses of percents (such as a 30% chance of rain or 80% on a test)?

- How do students understand, interpret, and use unit fractions? Can they explain why $1/10$ is smaller than $1/8$? Do they extend this reasoning to fractions with numerators greater than 1?

Investigation 2: Models for Fractions

- How do students represent common fractions as rotation around a circle?

- What strategies do students use to partition strips of paper into halves, thirds, fourths, sixths, and fifths? Do they fold the strips? Do they estimate and adjust? Do they measure? Do they use relationships between halves and fourths? between thirds and sixths?

- How do students find and use equivalent fractions and percents when they play fraction games?

- What strategies do students use to order fractions? Do they use percent equivalents? landmarks such as $1/2$ and 1? Can they sort fractions into those greater and less than $1/2$?

- How do students use the clock model to add fractions? How do students use the fraction strips?

Investigation 3: Exploring Decimals

- How accurately do students represent a decimal on a grid? What strategies do they use? How do they add decimals that are represented on the grid? What strategies do they use?

- How do students read and write decimals?

- What approaches do students use to order decimals? How do they reason about which is larger or smaller? (For example, do they recognize that .435 is less than .46 because .46 is the same as .460?)

- How comfortable are students with dividing to find decimal equivalents of fractions? Do they use answers from one problem to solve another? ($1/4$ = .25, so $3/4$ = .75) equivalents? ($1/2$, $2/4$, $3/6$, $4/8$, $5/10$, and $6/12$ are all .5) patterns?

- How do students compare fractions? What tools, models, and notations do they use?

- How do students interpret and make sense of word problems involving fractions, decimals, and/or percents? What strategies do they use to solve them?

Investigation 4: Data and Percents in Circle Graphs (Excursion)

- How do students go about planning and conducting their surveys? How do they formulate hypotheses? How do they choose and clarify a survey question? How do they decide on a plan for collecting data?

- How do students compile, organize, and represent their survey data? How do they understand and use circle graphs? How do they use familiar fractions and percents? How do they interpret their results?

- What knowledge and reasoning do students use to interpret common uses of fractions, decimals, and percents?

In the *Investigations* curriculum, mathematical vocabulary is introduced naturally during the activities. We don't ask students to learn definitions of new terms; rather, they come to understand such words as *factor* or *area* or *symmetry* by hearing them used frequently in discussion as they investigate new concepts. This approach is compatible with current theories of second-language acquisition, which emphasize the use of new vocabulary in meaningful contexts while students are actively involved with objects, pictures, and physical movement.

Listed below are some key words used in this unit that will not be new to most English speakers at this age level, but may be unfamiliar to students with limited English proficiency. You will want to spend additional time working on these words with your students who are learning English. If your students are working with a second-language teacher, you might enlist your colleague's aid in familiarizing students with these words before and during this unit. In the classroom, look for opportunities for students to hear and use these words. Activities you can use to present the words are given in the appendix, Vocabulary Support for Second-Language Learners (p. 128).

larger, smaller *Larger* and *smaller* are used throughout the unit to describe fractions, decimals, and percents of greater and lesser value than a given reference.

halfway When students use the number line model for fractions, they recognize a point *halfway* across each line as representing fraction equivalents for ½.

male, female, children, adults In the fourth investigation, students do observational surveys to find the percentages of the participants in a particular activity that are *female* as opposed to *male* or that are *children* as opposed to *adults*.

Multicultural Extensions for All Students

Whenever possible, encourage students to share words, objects, customs, or any aspects of daily life from their own cultures and backgrounds that are relevant to the activities in this unit. For example, invite students to show how fractions, percents, and decimals are written differently in some parts of the world. They might also bring in examples of these three kinds of numbers found in newspapers or on product packaging in other languages or from other countries.

Investigations

INVESTIGATION 1

Exploring Percents and Fractions

What Happens

Session 1: Connecting Fractions, Decimals, and Percents Students discuss common uses of fractions, decimals, and percents and their meanings. Then, in pairs, they solve a set of word problems and discover how much they already know about fractions, decimals, and percents.

Session 2: Percent Grid Patterns As students explore further the connection between fractions and percents, they use fractions to describe a portion of a group. They then represent ½ of a group as 50 percent and discuss the meaning of *percent*. They color 10-by-10 grids in different patterns to represent percents and use these colored grids to find equivalent fractions.

Sessions 3 and 4: Fraction and Percent Grids Students color more 10-by-10 grids, this time to represent common fractions (thirds, fourths, fifths, sixths, and eighths); they then find the equivalent percents.

Sessions 5 and 6: Percent Equivalents Strips Students mark a paper strip of percents to show equivalent fractions. They use their strip as a reference for the In-Between Game, in which they develop their sense of the relative size of fractions as they lay out fraction cards in order.

Session 7: Fraction and Percent Problems Students use fractions and percents as they solve word problems. Afterward they discuss the problems and share their strategies for finding solutions.

Mathematical Emphasis

- using fractions to describe how many in a group share a particular characteristic
- representing fractions and percents on a number line
- finding equivalent fractions and percents
- ordering fractions and percents
- interpreting common uses of percent
- illustrating and identifying percents on 10-by-10 grids
- using ½ and 1 as references in ordering fractions and percents
- building on knowledge of unit fractions to use fractions with numerators greater than 1

What to Plan Ahead of Time

Materials

- Four-function calculators (available throughout the unit)
- Chart paper (Session 1)
- Colored pencils, crayons, or markers: 1 per student (Sessions 2–4)
- Scissors: 1 per small group (Sessions 5–6)
- Envelopes or resealable plastic bags for storing decks of cards (Sessions 5–6)
- Overhead projector, overhead pens (Sessions 2–6)

Other Preparation

- Duplicate student sheets and teaching resources (located at the end of this unit) in the following quantities. If you have Student Activity Booklets, copy only the items marked with an asterisk.

For Session 1

Family letter* (p. 131): 1 per student

Student Sheet 1, What Do You Already Know? (p. 132): 1 per student

Student Sheet 2, Everyday Uses of Fractions, Decimals, and Percents (p. 134): 1 per student (homework)

For Session 2

Student Sheet 3, Grid Patterns (p. 135): 1 per student and 1 transparency

Student Sheet 4, What Fraction Do You See? (p. 136): 1 per student (homework)

Grids (p. 178): 1–2 sheets per student and 1 transparency*

For Sessions 3–4

Student Sheet 5, Fraction and Percent Equivalents (p. 137): 1 per student

Student Sheet 6, Seeing Fractions and Percents on Grids (p. 138): 1 per student (homework)

Student Sheet 7, Grouping Equivalent Fractions (p. 139): 1 per student (homework)

Grids (p. 178): 3–5 sheets per student (homework) and 1 transparency*

For Sessions 5–6

Student Sheet 8, How to Play the In-Between Game (p. 140): 1 per student (class) and 1 per student (homework)

Percent Equivalents Strips* (p. 144): 1 strip per student and 1 transparency

Completed Percent Equivalents Strips* (p. 145): 1 strip per small group, and 1 per student (homework)

Fraction Cards (p. 146): 1 deck per pair (on card stock), and 1 per student (homework)

For Session 7

Student Sheet 9, Fraction and Percent Problems (p. 141): 1 per student

Student Sheet 10, $2/3$ and $3/4$ (p. 143): 1 per student (homework)

- Prepare an Equivalents chart, listing the following twenty numbers down the left side, large enough so they are easily read:

$$1 \quad \frac{1}{2} \quad \frac{1}{3} \frac{2}{3} \quad \frac{1}{4} \frac{3}{4} \quad \frac{1}{5} \frac{2}{5} \frac{3}{5} \frac{4}{5}$$

$$\frac{1}{6} \frac{5}{6} \quad \frac{1}{8} \frac{3}{8} \frac{5}{8} \frac{7}{8} \quad \frac{1}{10} \frac{3}{10} \frac{7}{10} \frac{9}{10}$$

- Cut apart the three sheets of Fraction Cards. (Note: Heavy lines indicate bottoms of cards when cut apart.) Store each deck in an envelope or resealable plastic bag. Only the 22 diamond (♦) cards are used in Investigation 1.
- Try a few rounds of the In-Between Game to be sure you understand how to play (directions on Student Sheet 8).
- Folders for students are recommended as students will be using several sheets for reference throughout the unit.

Connecting Fractions, Decimals, and Percents

Materials

- Chart paper
- Student Sheet 1 (1 per student)
- Student Sheet 2 (1 per student, homework)
- Family letter (1 per student)
- Four-function calculators (available)

What Happens

Students discuss common uses of fractions, decimals, and percents and their meanings. Then, in pairs, they solve a set of word problems and discover how much they already know about fractions, decimals, and percents. Their work focuses on:

- interpreting common uses of fractions, decimals, and percents
- expressing the same quantity as a fraction, decimal, and percent

Fractions, Decimals, and Percents

On chart paper, start three lists headed as follows:

Everyday Uses	*Everyday Uses*	*Everyday Uses*
of Fractions	*of Decimals*	*of Percents*

All through this unit, we're going to be using fractions, decimals, and percents. Let's start by listing some examples of ways we use these kinds of numbers.

As students suggest uses, record them under the appropriate heading. If they give only a number, ask them to give a real-world context for its use. If they have difficulty doing this, make your own suggestions.

You've suggested that point 1, or 1 tenth, is a decimal—where might you see this sort of number used? I know one place: on a car odometer—the meter that shows how many miles the car has traveled. Who can think of another use of decimals?

If students suggest only a general usage of percent, such as "in weather reports" or "telling how many people like different flavors of ice cream," help them assign a number to that idea; for example, "a 30 percent chance of rain" or "75 percent of preschoolers prefer vanilla."

Plan to keep these lists posted where they can be added to each day as students find more examples.

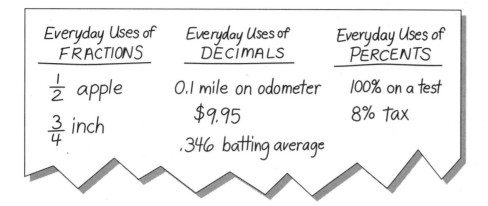

Everyday Uses of FRACTIONS

$\frac{1}{2}$ apple

$\frac{3}{4}$ inch

Everyday Uses of DECIMALS

0.1 mile on odometer

$9.95

.346 batting average

Everyday Uses of PERCENTS

100% on a test

8% tax

When the class has suggested something for each list, ask them to compare the concepts.

In what way are fractions, decimals, and percents alike?

See if students understand that they are all ways of referring to parts of a whole, or different ways to show amounts less than 1, or amounts between two whole numbers.

Write one-half on the board in the three notations:

½   0.5   50%

What do you know about these three numbers? How are they the same? How are they different?

Although the fraction, decimal, and percent form are different ways of representing the same amount, a lot depends on the situation—in certain cases, one form may be more commonly used than the others. For example, batting averages are commonly expressed as a decimal, even though there are equivalent ways of stating the same idea using fractions and decimals:

His batting average was .500 last week.

He got a hit one-half (½) of the times he came to bat.

He got a hit 50% of the times he came to bat.

You might point out that in some situations, one form may not make sense. For example, we might talk about 0.5 inch, or ½ inch, but not 50% of an inch. A sale price might be advertised as ¼ off or 25% off, but not 0.25 off.

During this discussion, expect that students will vary in what they understand about the relationships among the three representations. Be alert to any misconceptions students might have, and plan to address these as the unit progresses. For a discussion of the benefits of dealing with all three forms at the same time, see the **Teacher Note**, About Teaching Fractions, Percents, and Decimals Together (p. 8).

Teacher Checkpoint

Showing What You Know

Note: For this activity and throughout the unit, students may use an ordinary four-function calculator. If you have fraction calculators, do not make them available before Investigation 3.

Students each complete their own copy of Student Sheet 1, What Do You Already Know? but they may discuss their work with a partner. One purpose of this activity is to help students realize how much they already know about fractions, percents, and decimals.

❖ **Tip for the Linguistically Diverse Classroom**   Pair English-proficient students with second-language learners. Encourage them to make sketches to help clarify unfamiliar words on the student sheet.

Observe students while they work to learn how they are thinking about the problems and to see in which areas the class will need more experience. Following are some questions to consider as you circulate:

- Do students answer the question in the form asked for? That is, do they provide a percent, a fraction, a decimal, or a whole number as the problem specifies?
- Can students express a portion of a number (2 out of 5) as a fraction ($2/5$)?
- Can students find the missing portion of a whole? (If we have $2/5$, we are missing $3/5$.)
- Do they understand that when we write money using a decimal point, we do not also use a cent sign? (That is, $.25 is correct; .25¢ is not. The latter could mean one fourth of 1¢, or 0.0025 of a dollar.)
- Can students interpret time given in decimals, and can they recognize which is the fastest time in a race?

- Do they know that fractions equal to 1 (n/n) can be split into $1/n$'s? For example, do they recognize that 5/5 equals 1 and that $1/5 + 1/5 + 1/5 + 1/5 + 1/5$ equals $5/5$? Do they know that $2/n$ is twice as much as $1/n$, and $3/n$ is three times as much?
- Do they understand that to find thirds, we break the total into three equal groups?
- Do they recognize the decimal 0.25 as one-fourth ($1/4$)?
- Do they know that 100% is a whole and 50% is a half?

When everyone has completed the sheet, bring students together to go over the problems, sharing what they know. Do not emphasize right and wrong answers, but focus on how they make sense of the fractions, decimals, and percents in the different situations.

Session 1 Follow-Up

Everyday Uses of Fractions, Decimals, and Percents Send home the family letter or the *Investigations* at Home booklet. Remember to sign the letter before copying it. Also send home Student Sheet 2, Everyday Uses of Fractions, Decimals, and Percents. Students look for examples at home to extend the lists they started in class. You might suggest that students look on the kitchen shelves as well as in newspapers, magazines, or on television. Ask students to record what they find on Student Sheet 2.

 **Homework**

Fractions, Decimals, and Percents Collage Students make a collage of fractions, decimals, and percents that they find in magazines, newspapers, or brochures.

 **Extension**

About Teaching Fractions, Percents, and Decimals Together

Fractions, percents, and decimals are all ways of showing numbers less than a whole. Each form has unique qualities that make it easier to use in certain situations. Being comfortable with all three leads to a richer understanding of each and better enables students to choose which one is appropriate for computing or communicating a particular idea. For example, a young adult would not say, "I've been in school point 75 (or 75 hundredths) of my life," but might say "I've been in school about three-quarters of my life," or "I've been in school for 75 percent of my life."

One premise of the *Investigations* curriculum is that students should become familiar with fractions, percents, and decimals as quantities, and that their strategies for doing computation with fractional amounts should be based on this knowledge. Sometimes, it makes sense to do computations mentally. In other cases, it makes sense to use a calculator. Students might readily find ¾ or 0.75 of 32 mentally (especially if they understand the equivalency of the decimal and the fraction), but would choose a calculator to multiply 0.75 by a less familiar or larger number. Both approaches are sound. What makes little sense is routinely following an algorithm, such as deriving percents from fractions by dividing the numerator by the denominator and multiplying by 100, without first considering the number involved.

Continued on next page

Students who have done the *Investigations* units at grades 3 and 4 have used whole-number landmarks—familiar round numbers like 20, 25, 50, 100, and 1000—as reference points in the computation of less familiar numbers. In this unit, they work with fractions in the same way, by building on what they know. That is, they build on their knowledge of halves to understand fourths and eighths; they use what they know about common fractions to help them understand mixed numbers; they use unit fractions (like 1/8) as a reference for fractions with numerators greater than 1 (like 5/8). They also think about the relationship between different fractions (say, thirds and sixths), and they order fractions according to size. As they invent their own methods of ordering fractions, they develop a sense of the relative magnitude of these numbers.

Since percents are easy to order, being familiar with percents helps students learn about the relative size of fractions. As they work with percents and fractions together, students begin to recognize that 3/8 is a little less than 4/10, and that 2/3, 3/4, and 5/6 are not all the same size, even though each is missing one piece from a whole.

Knowledge of relationships among common fractions and of factors of 100 provides a basis for developing knowledge of common percents and of relationships among them. For example 1/2 of 100 is 50, so 1/2 is 50%; 1/4 is half of a half, so its percent is half of 50%, and 3/4 = 1/4 + 1/4 + 1/4, so it is 25% + 25% + 25%, or 75%.

Decimals are easier than either percents or fractions to compute with, and it is easy to use the calculator for operations with decimals. However, the ease of computing with decimals is countered by the tendency to make errors in interpreting them or to avoid interpreting them at all.

Students often make errors with decimals because they treat them as if they are whole numbers, believing for example that a decimal with more digits denotes a larger quantity than one with fewer digits. They often simply "read the number" without relating the decimal to a quantity.

Being able to move easily between fractions and decimals helps build understanding, and, if students understand basic equivalencies, they can use an ordinary calculator to compute with fractions. For example, students can do such problems as 1/6 + 1/3 on the calculator by entering $0.1666666 + 0.3333333 = 0.4999999$, and know that the answer is 1/2; similarly, they can translate 3/4 × 82 to $0.75 \times 82 = 61.5$, and give the answer as 61 1/2.

Studying fractions, percents, and decimals together helps students build their number sense on a very deep level. They soon get a feel for the fact that 0.05 is not at all the same as 0.5, because they know that 0.5 is 1/2 or 50%, and 0.05 is only 1/20 or 5%. Knowledge of these relationships helps students estimate the result of calculations using any of these representations. It helps them catch computational errors, because they know what to expect about the size of a number. Finally, studying these ideas together gives students a better sense of how the different types of numbers are actually used in life, as well as in particular mathematical contexts.

Percent Grid Patterns

Materials

- Prepared Equivalents chart
- Grids transparency
- Student Sheet 3 (1 per student and 1 transparency)
- Grids (1–2 sheets per student)
- Colored pencils, crayons, or markers (at least 1 per student)
- Overhead projector and pens
- Student Sheet 4 (1 per student, homework)
- Four-function calculators (available)

What Happens

As students explore further the connection between fractions and percents, they use fractions to describe a portion of a group. They then represent ½ of a group as 50 percent and discuss the meaning of percent. They color 10-by-10 grids in different patterns to represent percents and use these colored grids to find equivalent fractions. Their work focuses on:

- using fractions to describe how many in a group share a particular characteristic
- partitioning a whole
- making patterns and identifying percents on 10-by-10 grids
- identifying equivalent fractions and percents

Activity

What Fraction Do You See?

Ask for six volunteers to stand before the rest of the class. Take a moment to identify, for yourself, some characteristics that some of the students have in common.

Some of these students share certain characteristics. *[Describe examples that fit your volunteers.]* **For example, some of them are wearing [blue], some are wearing [glasses], and some have [buttons on their shirts]. Let's make a list of things we can say about the characteristics some of the students share, making statements that show how many in the group share each characteristic.**

❖ **Tip for the Linguistically Diverse Classroom** So that everyone understands which characteristic is being discussed, point to the identifying feature—button, shirt, pair of glasses, and so forth—as you refer to it.

Choose a characteristic that more than one, but not all, of the six students share. Make a statement about the number of students in the group who share this characteristic, and record it on the board. For example:

Three of the six students at the front of the room are wearing buttons. *[Write that on the board.]* **Is there another way we could say this?**

Record students' ideas on the board. Possibilities include stating the number of students wearing buttons as a fraction or percent, or stating the number in the group who are not wearing buttons.

How could we describe the number of students wearing buttons as a fraction?

Many students will see three out of the six students as half a group and may suggest "½ of the students are wearing buttons." If necessary, also explain that another way to describe the situation is "³⁄₆ of the students are wearing buttons."

> 3 out of 6 students are wearing buttons.
> 3 out of 6 are not wearing buttons.
> 50% are wearing buttons.
> $\frac{3}{6}$ of the students are wearing buttons.
> Half the students are wearing buttons.

Encourage students to pick out other characteristics that they can describe with fractions.

What are some other things we could say about the students at the front of the room? State your idea in a way so that someone could tell how many people have the characteristic and how many do not.

When students are familiar with using "__ out of __" and fraction statements, play this as a game. Students may recognize this as a variation of the similar classification game Guess My Rule, in which players try to figure out the common characteristic, or attribute, of a set of people or objects. They will also be doing similar classifying in the Ten-Minute Math activities during this investigation.

Invite another group—with a different number of students—to stand in front of the class. Choose a characteristic and state the fraction sharing it as a clue to those who are trying to guess the characteristic. For example:

Two-sevenths of this group follow my rule. Look at them and think about what my rule could be.

Three-fifths of the group are wearing a certain color that I'm thinking of. What color could it be?

Repeat the game a few times with different groups of students, perhaps until each student has had a chance to stand at the front of the room. Using a group of a different size each time will make the denominators of the fractions different. You might invite students to take the lead in posing questions for others to guess.

Interpreting Percents

Take an example from the preceding activity to discuss the meaning of 50 percent.

When we recorded that 3 out of 6 students were [wearing buttons], we also said that 50 percent were [wearing buttons]. *[Write 50% on the board.]*

Let's talk about what *50 percent* **means. Does it always mean 3 people? What if there were 20 people and 50% were [wearing buttons]—how many would that be? What if there were 50 people? 100 people?**

Some students may know that 50 percent always means half the people, and that number will change, depending on how many people are in the whole group. Write the fractions that represent the above situations:

$\frac{3}{6}$	=	3 out of 6	=	50% =	$\frac{1}{2}$
$\frac{10}{20}$	=	10 out of 20	=	50% =	$\frac{1}{2}$
$\frac{25}{50}$	=	25 out of 50	=	50% =	$\frac{1}{2}$
$\frac{50}{100}$	=	50 out of 100	=	50% =	$\frac{1}{2}$

Explain that these expressions·are all *equivalent,* or equal to, 50 percent. Thus they are also equivalent to each other. Begin the class Equivalents chart with this example.

EQUIVALENTS

1

$\frac{1}{2} = 50\% = \frac{3}{6} = \frac{10}{20} = \frac{25}{50} = \frac{50}{100} = $ 50 out of 100 = 1 out of 2

$\frac{1}{3}$

$\frac{2}{3}$

$\frac{1}{4}$

Throughout the unit we will use this chart to record equivalents we find. Equivalents are fractions, percents, and decimals that represent the same amount—they are different ways of writing numbers that have the same value.

Explain to students that they will be adding to the chart throughout this unit. You may want to suggest that students also keep their own list of equivalents in their math notebook or folder.

Writing Percents as Fractions   Discuss the meaning of the word *percent* as "part per hundred."

The word *percent* means "out of 100." So, *50 percent* is like saying "50 out of 100," and we can write that as the fraction 50/100. One percent, then, means 1 part per hundred, or 1 out of 100. So how could we write 1 percent as a fraction?

Write 1/100 on the board. Explain that all percents can be written as a fraction with 100 as the denominator. Some can also be written more simply, with smaller numbers in the denominator. Ask students how to write some that can't be simplified and others that can; for example:

How would we write 87 percent as a fraction? How would we write 9 percent as a fraction? What about 10 percent? Who knows another way to write 10 percent as a fraction?

$$87\% = \frac{87}{100} \qquad 9\% = \frac{9}{100} \qquad 10\% = \frac{10}{100} = \frac{1}{10}$$

We already talked about some ways to write 50 percent as a fraction. *[Refer to the Equivalents chart.]* **Are there other fractions that mean the same as 50%?**

When talking about fractions with your students, use correct terms, such as *numerator* and *denominator*. If your students are not familiar with these terms, or if they frequently mix up the meanings, provide brief definitions along with the term. For example, you might say:

All percents can be written with 100 as the denominator—the bottom number in the fraction.

Model the correct use of terms, but do not insist that students use them. They will learn to use correct terms readily if you use these words naturally yourself and help students remember the terms when they forget.

Grid Patterns as Percents

Display a Grids transparency on the overhead.

How many squares are on one of these grids? How do you know?

If anyone compares these grids to 100 charts, acknowledge the similarity, but explain the difference: Instead of each small square representing 1, we will say that the large square—the whole grid—represents 1 whole, and this whole has been divided into 100 equal parts. So each small square represents $1/100$, or 1 percent, of the grid.

Display a transparency of Student Sheet 3, Grid Patterns, on the overhead with only the first pattern exposed.

Who has a quick estimate of the percent of the squares in this grid that are shaded?

Record students' estimates on the board, then give students time to figure out exactly how many and what percent of the squares are shaded.

Before you tell us your answer, share with us how you figured out how many squares, and what percent of the whole, are shaded.

Following are some strategies you might hear:

■ Adding 2 + 4 + 6 + 8 + 10 and doubling.
■ Counting squares in unshaded corners, multiplying by 4, and subtracting from 100.
■ Dividing the pattern into fourths, counting shaded squares, then multiplying by 4.

Review how the percent shaded in can be written as a fraction ($60/100$). A few students may know that since 6 of every 10 squares are shaded, the fraction can also be written as $6/10$ or even $3/5$. Encourage and record such solutions on the Equivalents chart if students suggest them.

Hand out Student Sheet 3, Grid Patterns. Under the first grid, students record the percent and all fractions they have found for the problem just discussed. Ask for quick estimates of the percent of shaded squares in each of the other grids. Record these estimates on the board. Students then determine the actual percent of squares that is shaded in grids 2–4. Encourage them to find ways other than counting each square to figure it out. Below each grid, they write the percent and the fraction that represents the shaded portion.

When you are writing the fraction that is shaded, write all the equivalent fractions you know that represent the percent that's shaded.

When students have finished, they share answers and their strategies. You may want to discuss the following:

- **Grid 2** (60%, 6/10, 3/5) How did they count or figure this pattern? Are they surprised that this pattern has the same percent of shaded squares as grid 1? Does one of the two grids look like it has a higher percent shaded?

- **Grid 3** (25%, 25/100, 1/4) In what different ways did they view this pattern? Students will probably mention that the pattern looks somewhat like a checkerboard. Suggest looking at the pattern as if they were reading—going left to right in each row and continuing on to the next row.

  How frequently is a square shaded? (Every fourth square, or 1 out of every 4 squares.) **What percent and fraction of the grid is shaded? What common fraction is equivalent to 25/100? Is there an easy way to see that 1/4 of the squares are shaded?**

  You might also ask:

  If 1 out of every 5 squares were shaded, what fraction would that represent? What percent? What if 3 out of every 10 squares were shaded?

- **Grid 4** (36%, 36/100) How did they count or figure out this pattern? How did they count the half squares?

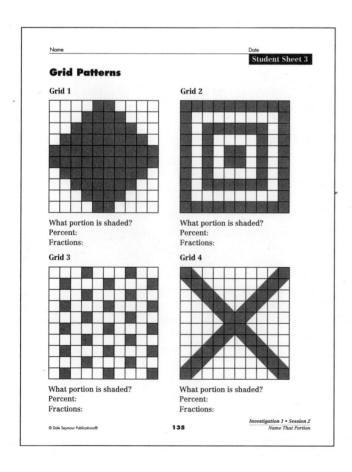

Making Grid Patterns

Distribute copies of the Grids sheet. Using colored pencils, crayons, or markers, students color in their own patterns and find the percent of the whole grid they have colored. They also record the percent as a fraction (with 100 as the denominator), and, if they know one, an equivalent fraction. Make additional copies of the student sheet available for students who finish early and would like to explore further. For example, they might want to try representing a particular percent with different patterns.

Students cut out each completed pattern, writing their name and the percent colored on the back. These can be used for one or both of the following activities in small groups:

- Students exchange patterns and figure out the percent colored in on each others' grids.
- Groups pool their grids and order them according to the percent colored in.

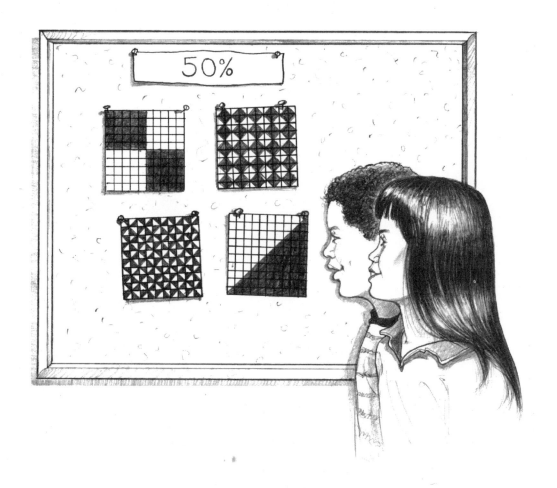

What Fraction Do You See? Students write at least three different statements about a small group of people—perhaps family members or friends—and record the fraction that represents each statement on Student Sheet 4, What Fraction Do You See? They illustrate their statements, drawing the group and exaggerating the features described. For example:

3 out of 5 have sneakers.
$\frac{2}{5}$ have glasses.
$\frac{1}{5}$ has a skirt on.
$\frac{1}{5}$ has straight hair.
$\frac{4}{5}$ have curly hair.

❖ **Tip for the Linguistically Diverse Classroom** Students may also use drawings in place of words in their written statements.

More Everyday Uses of Fractions, Decimals, and Percents Students continue to look for examples at home to extend the lists they started in class, Everyday Uses of Fractions, Decimals, and Percents. Challenge them to find examples that are written in the form "[3] out of [4]."

Percent and Fraction Patterns Students make more patterns to illustrate percents and fractions. After coloring a pattern on a grid, they identify the fraction and the percent on the back.

Fraction/Percent/Decimal Display Set up a bulletin board that shows different grid patterns for equivalent fractions, percents, and decimals. Challenge students to arrange their percent grids in order, putting different designs for the same amount below one another. To guide in the placement of the designs, you might post labels as titles—such as 0%, 50%, and 100%—with space between them for other percents. Students will continue coloring grids in the next activity and in Investigation 2; these, as well as other models of fractions, percents, and decimals, can be added to the bulletin board as work on the unit proceeds. Be sure students label all the grids on the back with their names and the percent and fraction colored.

Using the Grid Patterns The colored grid patterns from this unit might be collected in a box, and students could work individually or in pairs to put the collection in order. You could also save the grids for use in Investigation 2 as additional cards for the game Capture Fractions (see p. 60), with percent grids translated into equivalent fractions.

Fraction and Percent Grids

Materials

- Grids (3–5 sheets per student, homework)
- Grids transparency
- Student Sheet 5 (1 per student)
- Equivalents chart
- Colored pencils, crayons, or markers (at least 1 per student)
- Overhead projector and pens
- Student Sheet 6 (1 per student, homework)
- Student Sheet 7 (1 per student, homework)
- Four-function calculators (available)

What Happens

Students color more 10-by-10 grids, this time to represent common fractions (thirds, fourths, fifths, sixths, and eighths); they then find the equivalent percents. Their work focuses on:

- representing common fractions on 10-by-10 grids
- identifying equivalent fractions and percents

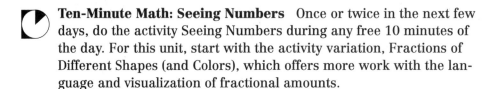 **Ten-Minute Math: Seeing Numbers** Once or twice in the next few days, do the activity Seeing Numbers during any free 10 minutes of the day. For this unit, start with the activity variation, Fractions of Different Shapes (and Colors), which offers more work with the language and visualization of fractional amounts.

Put a collection of five to ten small objects on the overhead—paper clips, erasers, pattern blocks, counting chips, magnetic letters or numbers, or plastic objects in familiar shapes—animals, trees, houses, people, boats, cars, and so forth. Include transparent shapes in colors if available.

Students take turns making statements that identify parts of the whole collection. Suggest that they start with "___ out of ___" statements, which they then express as fractions. For example:

3 out of 7 are paper clips; $3/7$ of the objects are paper clips.

2 out of 7 are round; $2/7$ of the objects are round.

To include all the students, you might allow time for them to work in pairs, making lists of statements about the collection. These can be shared in a brief discussion.

For full directions and other versions of Seeing Numbers, see p. 124.

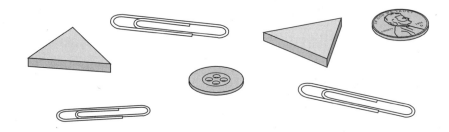

Fourths and Eighths on Grids

Display your Grids transparency on the overhead. Ask how you might color ¼ of the squares in a grid. If students suggest shading 1 out of every 4 squares (as in Grid 3 on Student Sheet 3, which they saw in Session 1), ask if there is a faster way to do it.

Invite a volunteer to come to the overhead and color in ¼ of the squares on one grid. Ask for another possibility. Then focus attention on one of the colored grids; ask how many squares are colored and record the colored portion as a fraction.

How can both ¼ and ²⁵⁄₁₀₀ represent the fraction for the amount of colored squares?

Listen to see if students understand the equivalence of the fractions. Some may mention that in both fractions the numerator is ¼ of the denominator, or show that 1 out of every 4 is the same as 25 out of every 100. Add any new information to your class chart of equivalents.

Ask how to color ²⁄₄ and then ³⁄₄ of the squares on another grid, and how to represent each amount as a fraction with a denominator of 100. Distribute a copy of Grids to each pair of students.

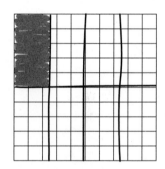

How many squares should we color to show ⅛? If you think you know, figure out how many squares would show ³⁄₈.

Students work in pairs to color ⅛ and ³⁄₈ of the squares. Let students know that it is fine to color in part of a square. Provide time for all students to color in ⅛ before sharing ideas.

When they are ready, students share different strategies for figuring out how to color ⅛ of the grid and how many squares need to be colored. Strategies might include the following.

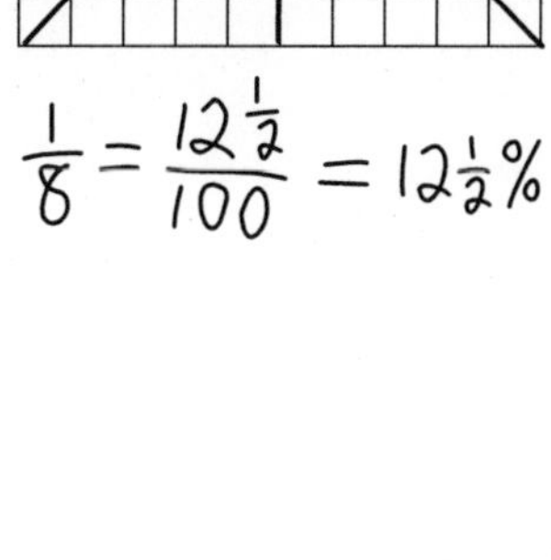

- ¼ is 25 squares, and ⅛ is half of a fourth, so that would be half of 25, or 12½ squares.
- 100 divided by 8 is 12½.
- Demonstrate on a grid by dividing it first into halves, then each half into halves, and finally each fourth into halves.

Throughout this activity, encourage students to use percents they know to find others. For example, ¼ is 25% so ²⁄₄ is 50% and ³⁄₄ is 75%; and ⅛ is half of a fourth, so it is 12½%. Reasoning from this, ²⁄₈ must be twice as much or 25%, and for ³⁄₈ they can add on one more 12½% to get 37½%.

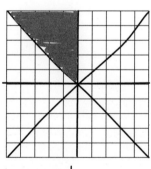

$$\frac{1}{8} = \frac{12\frac{1}{2}}{100} = 12\frac{1}{2}\%$$

Finding Fraction and Percent Equivalents

Distribute Student Sheet 5, Fraction and Percent Equivalents. Make copies of Grids available for students to take if they need them.

This page [Student Sheet 5] lists a number of common fractions in a chart of equivalents. Your job is to record the percent equivalent for each fraction given. The fractions equal to 100% are already recorded. Some of the others we have already found in class—write in the ones you recognize. Look for patterns in the chart to find other equivalencies. These fractions are the most challenging *[list them on the board]*:

$$\frac{1}{3} \quad \frac{2}{3}$$

$$\frac{1}{6} \quad \frac{2}{6} \quad \frac{4}{6} \quad \frac{5}{6}$$

$$\frac{1}{8} \quad \frac{3}{8} \quad \frac{5}{8} \quad \frac{7}{8}$$

Color in grids if that would help you. After you have colored part of a grid, write the fraction and its equivalent percent. Then record the percent on your chart of equivalents. After you have found a few of the percents by making grids, see if you can figure out some others *without* **coloring grids. Be ready to explain how you figured them out.**

Students may do the fractions in any order, working alone or with a partner. Suggest that when coloring grids, they start by shading lightly with a pencil; then, after checking their accuracy with a partner, they can use a crayon or marker to color in the fraction.

Circulate and observe students as they work. When they are using the grids, how do they figure out how many squares to color, particularly for the fractions that don't equal a whole number of squares? Encourage students to talk through their thinking about 1/3. For example, what number is 1/3 of 100? How can they use information about 1/3 to find percent equivalents for 2/3 and 1/6, *without* coloring more grids?

Note: In the first two investigations, use fractions (66⅔%), rather than decimals (66.67%) or rounding (67%) to represent equivalent percents for thirds and eighths. Also, at this point it makes more sense for students to talk about "one-half" rather than "point five" of a square. Decimal equivalents will be further explored later in the unit, in Investigation 3.

Encourage students to talk together in pairs or small groups, comparing their results and the strategies they used.

Discussion: Equivalent Fractions and Percents

When most of the students have made considerable progress on Student Sheet 5, bring the class together to discuss how they determined the percents for eighths, thirds, and sixths. The **Dialogue Box,** Finding Thirds and Sixths on the Grids (p. 23), illustrates some students' strategies for solving this kind of problem. Have a Grids transparency available for students to demonstrate how they used grids to figure out equivalents for such fractions as 3/8, 5/8, 1/3, 2/3, 1/6, or 5/6.

It is easier for most students to explain how 1/8 is 12 1/2% than how 1/3 is 33 1/3% or how 1/6 is 16 2/3%, because they find it easier to think about dividing a square in half than in thirds. It is important for students to make sense of these three particular percents since they are so commonly used. You may want to take time to discuss how to find 1/3 of 100. (For an example, read Yu-Wei's reasoning in the **Dialogue Box,** Finding Thirds and Sixths on the Grids, p. 23.)

What patterns did you see that helped you complete the chart of fraction and percent equivalents? How did you find percents for fractions when you didn't make grids? What strategies did you use?

■ Many students use their knowledge of money to help them with the fourths: "I know one-fourth, or 1 quarter, is 25%, just like money. It takes 4 quarters to make a dollar, so 3 out of 4 is the same as 3/4, or 75%."

■ Some students may notice patterns like the following: "I know 1/5 of 100 is 20 because five 20's make 100. So 2/5 is another 20 and that's 40, and 3/5 is another, and that's 60. It's like counting by 20's." Encourage them to think beyond the pattern they see. For example:

You're telling me that 1/5 is 20 percent, and you used that information to figure out other fifths fractions, like 2/5 and 3/5. Could you use it to tell me what the equivalent percent would be for 7/5?

■ Other students may see the above strategy in a more general way: "Going down each column, the percent is the smallest percent bigger every time." (For example, the eighths column increases by 12 1/2% each time.)

To prepare the students for the homework after Session 4, ask them to list fractions equivalent to 50 percent and to look for how these fractions are alike. If they see it only as a pattern "where the numbers on the top go up by 1's, and the ones on the bottom go up by 2's," probe their understanding of the relationship of the top number to the bottom number by asking them to use that pattern to fill in a missing numerator or denominator. For example, ask for a fraction that is equivalent to 50 percent with 16 as the denominator, or one with 10 in the numerator.

$$50\% = \frac{?}{16} = \frac{10}{?}$$

Challenge students to name other fractions equal to ¼. Start by writing parts of fractions on the board:

How many twentieths is one-fourth? [*Write* $\frac{?}{20}$]

Eleven of what is one-fourth? [*Write* $\frac{11}{?}$]

What if the denominator was 200? [*Write* $\frac{?}{200}$]

What if the denominator was 5?

[*Write* $\frac{?}{5}$, *and show students that it is fine to write* $\frac{1\frac{1}{4}}{5}$]

What if the numerator was 2½? [*Write* $\frac{2\frac{1}{2}}{?}$]

What are some other fractions equal to one-fourth?

Once students have had a chance to share and hear others' strategies, allow time for them to correct and add to their work on Student Sheet 5 for a few minutes before joining their neighbors to compare results. If there is time, students might add equivalents from this activity to the class Equivalents chart.

Sessions 3 and 4 Follow-Up

🏠 Homework

Seeing Fractions and Percents on Grids   After Session 3, students take home a copy of Student Sheet 6, Seeing Fractions and Percents on Grids, and find fraction and percent equivalents for two or three fractions they have not found in class.

Grouping Equivalent Fractions   After Session 4, students group equivalent fractions—fractions that are equal to the same percent. They record these on Student Sheet 7, Grouping Equivalent Fractions. For example:

$$50\% = \frac{1}{2} = \frac{2}{4} = \frac{3}{6} = \frac{4}{8} = \frac{5}{10}$$

Students might use a copy of the Grids sheet (p. 178) to help them with this task. Tell students they will need to bring Student Sheet 7 back to class the next day to use as a reference.

Finding Thirds and Sixths on the Grids

After working on the activity Finding Fraction and Percent Equivalents (p. 20), these students are sharing how they found different fractions.

Who wants to share how they figured out how much to shade in for one-third of the grid?

Rachel: I knew 25 squares was a fourth. So I tried 30, but that wasn't enough because I still had 10 squares left. I tried 32 squares, and that left 4 extra, so I tried 33. That left 1 extra square. So I had to divide that square into three parts.

Yu-Wei: Three times 3 is 9, so 3 times 30 would be 90. Then put 3 more on each 30 and that would be 99 since three 33's are 99. Then all you need to do is add $\frac{1}{3}$ to each 33.

How much is two-thirds of the grid?

Trevor: Two 33's is 66 and two $\frac{1}{3}$'s is $\frac{2}{3}$. That's $66\frac{2}{3}$ squares.

How about sixths? Does anyone want to tell us about a sixth?

Alani: Two-sixths make a third, and that's $33\frac{1}{3}$. Then to find half of $33\frac{1}{3}$, I know that half of a third is $\frac{1}{6}$. Half of 3 is $1\frac{1}{2}$, and half of 30 is 15. So that would be $16\frac{1}{2}$ plus $\frac{1}{6}$, whatever that is.

Does everybody agree that $\frac{2}{6}$ equals $\frac{1}{3}$? *[Julie goes to the board and draws a rectangle with six parts, shading in one-third.]*

Julie: See, I've colored in 2 out of the 6, so that is $\frac{2}{6}$. And it's also $\frac{1}{3}$ if you take away the middle line that goes across.

Who figured out sixths a different way?

Marcus: We cut up a grid. First we cut all the rows apart. That means we broke it up into 10 tenths. We took out six rows of those tenths and started six piles, because it's sixths. Now we had four rows left. We cut each of those rows in half and put 5 squares with each of the six rows. So now each of the sixths has 15 squares. Six batches of 15 came out to 90 of the 100 squares. Then we tried adding 2 squares to each pile, but it didn't work. That would take 12 squares. So we decided to add one more. Now each batch has 16 squares.

How many squares did they use so far? How many squares were left to divvy up? Can they give one more square to each of the six piles?

Robby: That made 96 squares. We took the last 4 squares and cut them in half, and gave a half to each pile.

Now how many in each pile? Toshi?

Toshi: There's $16\frac{1}{2}$.

Noah: But there's still 2 half-squares left—one piece for three of the piles, and the other piece for the other three piles.

Duc: We cut it in sixths. So each pile had 16 and a half squares, plus another $\frac{1}{6}$. Then we got stuck, just like Alani.

Look at Julie's drawing on the board. See if you can use it to help you add $16\frac{1}{2}$ and $\frac{1}{6}$. Take a minute to work with your group on this.

[The teacher circulates, then calls the class together. Greg uses Julie's rectangle with six parts to demonstrate how to add one-half and one-sixth.]

Greg: This is how we figured it. If you color in 3 squares on Julie's drawing, that's one-half, or 3 sixths, and 1 sixth more is 4 sixths.

Maricel: And $\frac{4}{6}$ is the same as $\frac{2}{3}$. Look! *[She points this out on Julie's drawing.]*

So what's the total for one-sixth? How many squares on the grid is one-sixth? What would the percent be?

Greg: It'd be $16\frac{4}{6}$—no, $16\frac{2}{3}$ percent.

Percent Equivalents Strips

Materials

- Percent Equivalents Strips (1 strip per student, and 1 transparency)
- Scissors (1 per small group)
- Completed Student Sheet 7 (from Sessions 3–4)
- Completed Percent Equivalents Strips (1 strip per small group and 1 per student, homework)
- Student Sheet 8 (2 per student; 1 for class, 1 for homework)
- Fraction Cards (1 deck per pair and 1 per student, homework)
- Overhead projector and pens
- Envelopes or resealable plastic bags
- Four-function calculators (available)

What Happens

Students mark a paper strip of percents to show equivalent fractions. They use their strip as a reference for the In-Between Game, in which they develop their sense of the relative size of fractions as they lay out fraction cards in order. Their work focuses on:

- finding equivalent fractions and percents
- ordering fractions and percents around landmark numbers

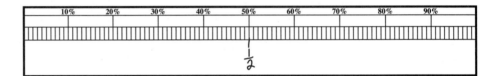

Activity

Teacher Checkpoint

Marking a Percent Equivalents Strip

Distribute scissors and one copy of the sheet of Percent Equivalents Strips to every four students. Groups cut out and share the strips so that each student has one.

Display a transparency of a Percent Equivalents Strip on the overhead.

Today you are going to put together what you have learned about fractions and percents to make a Percent Equivalents Strip like this. Every 10 percent is marked along the top, and the short, close-together lines show 1 percent. You need to mark where the common fractions go. For example, where would you mark for one-half?

Demonstrate where to write fractions on the strip by writing ½ directly under the line that indicates 50%. You may want to extend the 50% line down to show more clearly the relationship between the percent and fraction.

Write on the board the fractions students are to mark on the Percent Equivalents Strip.

halves   thirds   fourths   fifths   sixths   eighths

Tenths are not included because students know these percent-fraction equivalencies almost automatically; if some students want to include tenths on their strip, this is fine.

Write in only one fraction for a percent—there is not enough room on the strip to show all equivalent fractions. For example, ½, ²⁄4, ³⁄6, and ⁴⁄8 all are equal to 50 percent. Choose the most familiar fraction to write— the one expressed in lowest terms. So, in the case of 50 percent, write the fraction ½. We say that the fraction is "expressed in lowest terms" when both the numerator and the denominator are the smallest possible whole numbers for the fraction.

Note: Use the phrase "expressed in lowest terms" so students can become familiar with commonly used terminology, but don't expect students to use it. This curriculum does not use the phrase "reduce fractions" because it can be misleading—the word *reduce* seems to suggest that the fractions get smaller, which of course they don't.

For this activity, encourage students to work together and use whatever tools or references they find helpful. Observe students while they work, with the following points in mind:

- How do students identify the particular fractions they are to include on the strip—the halves, thirds, fourths, sixths, and eighths expressed in lowest terms? They might use their homework on Student Sheet 7, Grouping Equivalent Fractions, to find the fraction in each equivalent group that is in lowest terms. If some students are having trouble deciding which fractions to include on the strip, you may want to list the 15 specific fractions on the board:

$$\frac{1}{2} \quad \frac{1}{3} \quad \frac{2}{3} \quad \frac{1}{4} \quad \frac{3}{4} \quad \frac{1}{5} \quad \frac{2}{5} \quad \frac{3}{5} \quad \frac{4}{5} \quad \frac{1}{6} \quad \frac{5}{6} \quad \frac{1}{8} \quad \frac{3}{8} \quad \frac{5}{8} \quad \frac{7}{8}$$

- How do students find the location for each fraction on the strip? Do some students use fractional relationships? For example, do they place ¼ and ¾ at 25% and 75% immediately after placing ½ at 50% because they recognize the relationship between fourths and halves? Do some students need to refer each time to their Grouping Equivalent Fractions chart (Student Sheet 7)?

- Do students write each fraction at the correct location on the strip? Do they count the markings for multiples of 10 percent and the units to locate exactly where to write each fraction? Do they understand how to place fractions such as ⅓ and ⅛ that are not whole-number percents?

- When asked, how do students explain the sequential order of the fractions on the strip? For example, can students tell you that ⅜ is smaller than ⅖ because 37½% is smaller than 40%?

If students are making major errors, suggest that they discuss with neighbors some of the approaches they are using to mark the strips and why these approaches may or may not make sense.

When students have completed their Percent Equivalents Strips, distribute one Completed Percent Equivalents Strip to each group of four students. Students share these as they check their own strips and make them more precise. The students will be using these strips as reference tools throughout the unit, so have a few blank strips available for students who have made many errors and are determined to start over (but do not encourage this).

Playing the In-Between Game

Hand out a prepared deck of Fraction Cards to each pair of students. They take out the set of cards with diamonds (♦) to play the In-Between Game. Students also will need their completed Percent Equivalents Strips for reference during the game.

You might introduce this game by leading two students through a demonstration game, with the rest of the class grouped around to observe. Seat the two students side by side so both can easily see the cards on the table. In playing later, they will keep their dealt hands concealed from one another, but that is not necessary for the demonstration game since the observers will be able to see both hands.

The rules are given on Student Sheet 8, How to Play the In-Between Game. Refer to this sheet as needed while teaching the game. Decide whether or not you want to distribute the rules now for student use in class; in either case you will send them home with students to help them teach the game to their families.

The basic rules are as follows. Start by placing the three percent cards (10%, 50%, and 90%) spread apart in a row across the table (10% on the left, 90% on the right). (There should be plenty of room between the percent cards to place several fraction cards.) Shuffle the Fraction Cards and deal 6 to each player.

Players take turns placing one of their cards on the table. Each card placed must touch a card that is already on the table. Players may not place a card between two adjacent cards that are touching. Any card that is equivalent to one of the percent cards may be placed on top of the appropriate percent. At all times during the game, all the cards on the table must be in ascending order, from left to right. Play continues until neither player can place another card. The number of cards left in a player's hand is that player's score for the round. After five rounds, the player with the lowest score wins.

A sample round will illustrate how the game is played.

Jasmine is dealt these six cards:

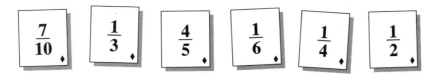

Maricel is dealt these six:

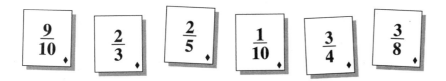

At the end of the round, the table looks like this:

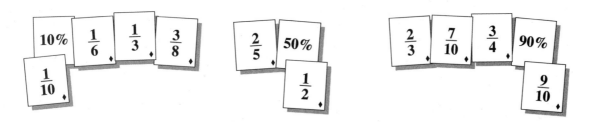

Jasmine has been unable to place ¼ and ⅘. She ends the round with a score of 2, while Maricel finishes with a score of 0.

Observing the Students   When students understand the rules, they play the In-Between Game in pairs. Circulate and observe students as they play.

■ How are they figuring out equivalent fractions and percents? Are they using their Percent Equivalents Strip? Do they automatically know the percent equivalents for some fractions?

■ Are students monitoring and checking each other's play?

■ Are students developing strategies as they play the game?

Variations

■ Students might enjoy playing a collaborative version with their cards exposed, working together so that both players place all their cards.

■ Challenge students to play without referring to their Percent Strips.

■ Pairs stop after a game and ask another team to check their work.

■ Students might post their game on a transparency. You can then use a few examples to analyze some sample rounds with students.

At the end of the session, students return the Fraction Cards to their storage envelope or bag for use in later investigations. They should also save their Percent Equivalent Strips for playing this game again, and for future reference.

Note: If you think your students might find this game difficult, you might postpone this game until after they experience the game Roll Around the Clock in Investigation 2.

Sessions 5 and 6 Follow-Up

 **Homework**

The In-Between Game   Students take home Student Sheet 8, How to Play the In-Between Game, along with Fraction Cards. They will also need a copy of the Completed Percent Equivalents Strips for reference.

If students might not have scissors at home, allow class time for them to cut apart the Fraction Cards. Although students need only the 22 diamond cards for this game, they will be playing other games at home later in the unit, and it generally works best to send home the entire deck at once. If possible, provide envelopes or resealable plastic bags for storage of the cards. Be sure students understand that they will soon be learning other games that use all the Fraction Cards, and advise them to find a safe place to keep them at home so the cards don't get lost.

Students are to teach the In-Between Game to their families and play several rounds. Advise students to be patient teachers. After playing the game in class, they may know the fraction and percent equivalents better than many adults.

Fraction and Percent Problems

What Happens

Students use fractions and percents as they solve word problems. Afterward they discuss the problems and share their strategies for finding solutions. Student work focuses on:

- naming portions with fractions and percents
- using 1/2 and 1 as references in ordering fractions and percents
- building on knowledge of unit fractions to use fractions with numerators greater than 1

Materials

- Student Sheet 9 (1 per student)
- Student Sheet 10 (1 per student, homework)
- Four-function calculators (available)
- Students' Percent Equivalents Strips (from Sessions 5–6)

Activity

Assessment

Fraction and Percent Problems

Students work individually on Student Sheet 9, Fraction and Percent Problems. They may use calculators, their Percent Equivalents Strips (as a reference), and pictures or drawings. Avoid recommending the use of any particular material; encourage them to use whatever helps them make sense of these problems.

❖ **Tip for the Linguistically Diverse Classroom** Before students begin work, pair English-proficient students with second-language learners to read aloud each problem as needed. As necessary, students can add sketches to the sheet to help with unfamiliar vocabulary.

Circulate while students are working and observe how they are thinking about the problems. Following are the answers, along with some questions and issues to consider as you evaluate student work:

- **Problem 1 answers: (a)** 50% **(b)** 25% **(c)** 12½% **(d)** 12½%

  Consider: Do students use the answers they find for one question to help them solve the problems that follow it? Do they recognize that the percents they find add up to 100 percent, which represents 40 students or one whole class?

- **Problem 2 answers will vary.**

  Consider: **(a)** Can students name four fractions? Can they show convincingly that they are greater than $\frac{1}{2}$ and less than one whole? Can they put their four fractions in order? **(b)** Because percents greater than 1 may not have come up in class, see if students know that any percent over 100 is greater than 1. **(c)** Do students know they are looking for percents between 25% and 50%? Do they realize that any number between 25% and 50% is correct, not just the familiar percents they have been working with, such as 30% and $37\frac{1}{2}$%?

- **Problem 3 answers: (a)** Sonya's are bigger. **(b)** Adam ate more, because $\frac{4}{10}$ is larger than $\frac{3}{8}$. Students may compare the two fractions in a variety of ways, including the Percent Equivalents Strip.

  Consider: Do students know that eighths are bigger than tenths? Can they show how they know? To help students figure out who ate the most, you might ask: "What fraction was each of Sonya's slices? each of Adam's slices? What percent of the whole loaf did Sonya eat? What percent did Adam eat? Which fraction is larger, $\frac{3}{8}$ or $\frac{4}{10}$?"

- **Problem 4 answers will vary, based on the size of your class.**

  Consider: Can students find 25 percent of the class? Do they divide by four, or do they find half of the class and then half of that? To find 75 percent, do they multiply the answer for (a) by 3, or do they subtract the answer for (a) from the class total?

  Are they sensible about providing a range, or using the word *about?* For example, in a class of 34 students, 25 percent is 8 or 9. Students who multiply that answer by 3 will come up with a range of 24 to 27 students. Those who subtract will get a narrower range of 25 to 26.

- **Problem 5 answers: (a)** 25 walked. **(b)** 50 walked. **(c)** $\frac{3}{4}$ of 100 did not walk, and $\frac{3}{4}$ of 200 did not walk. **(d)** 75 of the 100 did not walk, and 150 of the 200 did not walk.

  Consider: Can students find $\frac{1}{4}$ of 100? Can they use that answer to find $\frac{1}{4}$ of 200? Do students recognize that the answer to (c) is the same for both 100 and 200 people? Do they understand that the *fraction* of people who did not walk remains the same, while the *number* of people who did not walk changes?

- **Problem 6 answer:** Yes, if Rudy's was more than twice as large as Eli's pizza.

  Consider: Do students realize that how large the percent (or amount of pizza) is depends on the size of the whole? If students are having trouble, suggest that they try to draw the situation.

When students have finished, discuss the problems and their strategies for finding solutions. During this discussion, keep in mind the issues listed above. Collect students' papers for further assessment.

Session 7 Follow-Up

Homework

2/3 and 3/4 Students complete the following writing task on Student Sheet 10, 2/3 and 3/4:

> Write what you know about the fractions $\frac{2}{3}$ and $\frac{3}{4}$.
>
> Write at least three statements about each fraction.
>
> Then write three reasons you know $\frac{3}{4}$ is larger than $\frac{2}{3}$.

Student responses might include statements like these:

> $\frac{2}{3}$ is $\frac{1}{3}$ plus $\frac{1}{3}$.
>
> $\frac{2}{3}$ is $\frac{1}{3}$ away from a whole.
>
> $\frac{3}{4}$ is $\frac{1}{4}$ away from a whole.
>
> $\frac{2}{3}$ is $66\frac{2}{3}$%.

Or, they might write more specific statements:

> $\frac{2}{3}$ of a 100 grid is $66\frac{2}{3}$ squares.
>
> $\frac{3}{4}$ of a day is 18 hours.
>
> $\frac{2}{3}$ of 15 is 10.

Students' comparisons might be based on their statements about the individual fractions. For example:

> $\frac{2}{3}$ is $\frac{1}{3}$ away from a whole. $\frac{3}{4}$ is only $\frac{1}{4}$ away from a whole. And $\frac{1}{4}$ is smaller than $\frac{1}{3}$.
>
> $\frac{2}{3}$ is $66\frac{2}{3}$% and $\frac{3}{4}$ is 75%.
>
> $\frac{2}{3}$ of a day is 16 hours. $\frac{3}{4}$ of a day is 18 hours.
>
> If you eat $\frac{2}{3}$ you leave a bigger piece so $\frac{2}{3}$ is a littler piece than $\frac{3}{4}$.

INVESTIGATION 2

Models for Fractions

What Happens

Sessions 1 and 2: Fractions on Clocks   In this fraction model, students find fractions that represent the rotation of one hand around a clock face. They play a game, Roll Around the Clock, solving fraction addition problems. Finally, they write fraction addition and subtraction problems for classmates to solve.

Session 3: Fraction Strips   Students now work with a linear fraction model as they partition paper strips into halves, thirds, fourths, sixths, and, as a challenge, fifths. They use the strips as they look for ways that they can add two fractions together to equal a third fraction.

Sessions 4 and 5: Fraction Tracks   Students complete a set of Fraction Tracks, another linear model, showing all fractions between 0 and 1 for halves, thirds, fourths, fifths, sixths, eighths, and tenths. Students look for fraction equivalents and write about patterns they see. They count by fractions across the Fraction Track gameboard, a set of number lines from 0 to 2. Working in groups, students order fractions by size and play the game Capture Fractions.

Session 6: The Fraction Track Game   Students play the Fraction Track Game, turning over Fraction Cards to determine their total move. As the students put together different amounts to equal the fraction turned up, they discover how fractions can be broken into parts with unlike denominators.

Sessions 7 and 8: Fraction Games   During Choice Time, students play two or three of the fraction games they have already learned: the In-Between Game, Roll Around the Clock, the Fraction Track Game, and Capture Fractions.

Session 9: Problems with Fractions   Students solve word problems using fractions and percents and later share their solution strategies.

Mathematical Emphasis

- representing fractions as rotation around a circle
- marking strips into fractional parts
- finding equivalent fractions
- ordering fractions
- adding fractions

What to Plan Ahead of Time

Materials

- Fraction cubes, in two colors: 2 per pair (Sessions 1–2, 7–8)
- Chips, buttons, or small counters to use as game pieces: 20 per group of 3–4 students (Sessions 6–8; optional for Sessions 1–2)
- Overhead projector and pen (Sessions 1–2, 4–6)
- Chart paper (Sessions 1–5)
- Pencils (Session 3)
- Transparent tape, scissors (Sessions 4–5)
- Ruler: 1 per student (Sessions 4–5)
- Fraction Cards from Investigation 1: 1 deck per group of 3–4 students (Sessions 4–8)
- Class charts and Percent Equivalents Strips from Investigation 1 (Sessions 4–5; 7–8)

Other Preparation

- Duplicate student sheets and teaching resources (located at the end of this unit) in the following quantities. If you have Student Activity Booklets, copy only the items marked with an asterisk.

  For Sessions 1–2
  Student Sheet 11, Clock Fractions (p. 149): 1 per student

  Student Sheet 12, Clock Fractions Addition Problems (p. 150): 1 per student (homework)

  Large Clock Face* (p. 158): 1 transparency and several copies

  For Session 3
  Student Sheet 13, Fraction Strip Subtraction Problems (p. 151): 1 per student (homework)

  For Sessions 4–5
  Student Sheet 14, How to Play Capture Fractions (p. 152): 1 per student (homework)

  Fraction Track Gameboard (p. 159): 1 per student, and a transparency of page 1*

  For Session 6
  Student Sheet 15, How to Play the Fraction Track Game (p. 153): 1 per student (homework)

  Fraction Track Gameboard, page 1 (p. 159): 1 transparency

  For Sessions 7–8
  Student Sheet 16, More Everyday Uses of Fractions, Decimals, and Percents (p. 154): 1 per student (homework)

  For Session 9
  Student Sheet 17, Fractions of Pizza (p. 155): 1 per student

  Student Sheet 18, Moves on the Fraction Track (p. 157): 1 per student (homework)

- Before Session 1, prepare your fraction cubes with a sticker on each face. Write these fractions on the cubes:

  Cube 1: $\frac{1}{12}$ $\frac{1}{6}$ $\frac{1}{4}$ $\frac{1}{3}$ $\frac{5}{12}$ $\frac{1}{2}$

  Cube 2: $\frac{1}{2}$ $\frac{7}{12}$ $\frac{2}{3}$ $\frac{3}{4}$ $\frac{5}{6}$ $\frac{11}{12}$

- For Session 3, use a paper cutter and paper in five different colors to prepare fraction strips. Make the strips 8½ inches long by about 1 inch wide. Make a set of five strips, one of each color, for each student.

- After Session 5, fill in the missing fractions on your transparency of the Fraction Track Gameboard, page 1, to use as you introduce the game.

- Because students will take home their own Fraction Track Gameboards, assemble additional gameboards (1 per 3–4 students) for small group use in Sessions 7–8. First fill in a copy of Gameboard, page 1 (p. 159), then make the copies you need.

Materials

- Overhead projector (optional)
- Large Clock Face (transparency and extra copies)
- Equivalents chart
- Student Sheet 11 (1 per student)
- Fraction cubes (set of 2 per pair)
- Game chips (optional, 1 per student)
- Chart paper
- Student Sheet 12 (1 per student, homework)

Fractions on Clocks

What Happens

In this fraction model, students find fractions that represent the rotation of one hand around a clock face. They play a game, Roll Around the Clock, solving fraction addition problems. Finally, they write fraction addition and subtraction problems for classmates to solve. Their work focuses on:

- representing fractions as rotation around a circle
- adding fractions

Activity

Clock Fractions

Ask students to look at the clock on the wall. If you don't have a round wall clock, show the Large Clock Face transparency on the overhead.

Pretend that the minute hand on this clock is broken. The broken hand always points to 12. The hour hand still moves around to show the time. When the hour hand moves from 12:00 to 1:00, what fraction of the way around has it gone? ($\frac{1}{12}$) **Why is it $\frac{1}{12}$?**

To encourage students to think of this as a model of rotation rather than area, demonstrate the turn with your hand.

When the hour hand moves from 12:00 to 3:00, what fraction of the way around has it gone?

Some students may call the fraction one-fourth ($\frac{1}{4}$), and others may say three-twelfths ($\frac{3}{12}$). If students suggest more than one fraction, ask them to explain how both describe that turn. Add $\frac{3}{12}$ to the class Equivalents chart, beside $\frac{1}{4}$.

Imagine now that the hour hand is broken and the minute hand moves. When the minute hand moves from the 12 to the 3, how many minutes have gone by? What fraction is that of an hour, or 60 minutes?

Students may say that it is the same as the hour hand moving from 12:00 to 3:00, or $\frac{1}{4}$. Some might suggest that it is also $\frac{15}{60}$. If no one suggests this fraction, try to elicit it:

If we think of this problem in terms of minutes, there is another equivalent fraction. How many minutes has the hand moved *out of* the number of minutes in an hour? How do we write this fraction?

When students have identified the fraction 15/60, add it to the class Equivalents chart.

Now challenge the students to find representations for ⅓ on the clock.

This time, let's say the hand starts at the 12 and moves one-third of the way around the clock face. Where would the hand end up? Think about how many hours out of 12 the hand has moved—what fraction represents ⅓? (4/12) Now think about how many minutes out of 60 the hand moved—what fraction represents ⅓ in this sense? (20/60)

Distribute a copy of Student Sheet 11, Clock Fractions, to each student. Explain that the arrows inside the clocks show the rotation of one hand. Students are to write fractions that tell how far the hand has moved. Under each clock, they write all the fraction names they know for that particular interval (equivalent fractions). They do not need to do the clocks in any particular order.

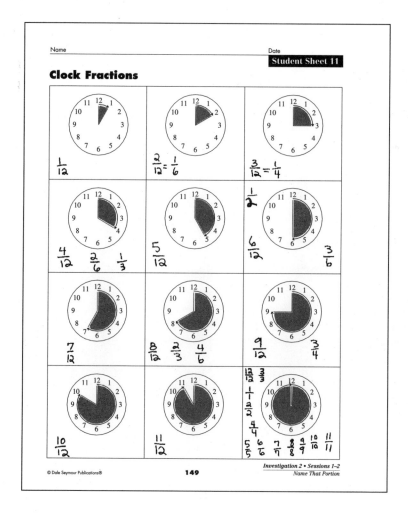

Circulate and observe students while they work. What strategies are they using to find fractions of the full circle?

As students find fractions, write them on the board in no particular order. There are 21 possible fractions, expressed in terms of halves, thirds, fourths, sixths, and twelfths less than 1; there are 12 more if students also think of sixtieths. If students stop before they have found many of the fractions, write on the board some of the fractions that no one has yet found and challenge them to figure out where they belong (to what fractions are they equivalent?).

Point out that all fractions that name the same amount are equivalent. Encourage students to make additions to your Equivalents chart. Students will need to think of each fraction in lowest terms to determine which set of fractions to write it with.

Activity

Adding Fractions on the Clock

Draw attention again to the class clock or to the Large Clock Face transparency on the overhead.

Now let's use the clock face to *add* fractions. Say the hand moved one-third of the way around the clock, and then it moved one-sixth more. Where will it end up? What fraction has it moved altogether?

Write the problem on the board:

$$\frac{1}{3} + \frac{1}{6} =$$

Encourage students to talk together and find more than one way to think about the problem. Some might find it helpful to look at the clock faces on their completed Student Sheet 11.

Students then share their approaches with the whole class. Some students may want to demonstrate their thinking using the Large Clock Face transparency. Look for different ways of thinking about the problem. If one student explains it in terms of hours, ask if anyone thought of it in minutes. Here are examples of these different ways of thinking about the problem:

> *[Thinking about hours]* I looked on my Clock Fractions sheet and saw that ⅙ is 2 hours and ⅓ is 4 hours, and 2 and 4 make 6. Six is halfway around.

> *[Thinking about minutes]* I knew that ⅙ is 10 minutes and ⅓ is 20 minutes, so together they make 30 minutes; that's half an hour.

On chart paper, start a list of fraction addition problems. Write the equation students just solved.

$$\frac{1}{3} + \frac{1}{6} = \frac{1}{2}$$

Write a few more examples on the board for students to do. For example:

$$\frac{1}{4} + \frac{1}{2} = \qquad \frac{1}{4} + \frac{1}{3} =$$

As you circulate, ask students to explain how they found the answers. Elicit different strategies and approaches. If some students finish quickly, you may want to include a more challenging problem, with numbers greater than 1.

How could you add 1¾ and 2⁵/₁₂ using the clock? *[Write the problem on the board.]*

$$1\frac{3}{4} + 2\frac{5}{12} =$$

Encourage students to work together on these problems and share with other students their strategies for finding the answer.

When using the clock model to add fractions, there is no need to convert fractions to a common denominator; this happens automatically. For example, when adding ¼ + ⅓, a student might reason this way:

> Moving ¼ of the way around is 3 o'clock. Moving ⅓ is 4 hours more, or 7 o'clock. That's equivalent to moving ⁷/₁₂ of the way around the clock.

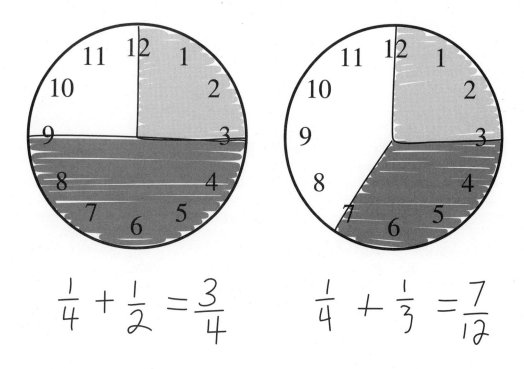

$$\frac{1}{4} + \frac{1}{2} = \frac{3}{4} \qquad \frac{1}{4} + \frac{1}{3} = \frac{7}{12}$$

Activity

Roll Around the Clock Game

Teach students how to play Roll Around the Clock. Read the directions and play the game once yourself first. Students play with a partner or in groups of three. Two pairs can also play together. Each group needs two prepared fraction cubes, preferably in different colors. The fractions on one cube should be one-half and less: 1/12, 1/6, 1/4, 1/3, 5/12, and 1/2. On the second cube, they are one-half and greater: 1/2, 7/12, 2/3, 3/4, 5/6, and 11/12. Students might also have their completed Student Sheet 11, Clock Fractions, to use for reference.

The object of the game is to roll fractions that sum to 1. To find the sum of the fractions rolled, some students may find it helpful to move a game piece, such as a button, around a copy of the Large Clock Face; make these materials available only as needed.

Players take turns. On a turn, a player may take one, two, three, or more rolls (of a single cube). For each roll, the player chooses which cube to roll. For example, a player might first choose to roll the cube with the larger fractions. Then, depending on the result, that player might (1) roll the cube with smaller fractions, (2) roll the larger fractions again, or (3) not roll at all.

If a player takes a second roll, the player may stop there, or take a third roll with either cube. The goal for each turn is to come as close as possible to 1, adding the results of all rolls. This is similar to the game of Twenty-One, but in Roll Around the Clock, players do not lose when they exceed the goal number of 1.

On a sheet of paper, students record the fractions they roll in the form of an equation. For example, a player who rolls 1/3 and 3/4 would record it this way:

$$\frac{1}{3} \; + \; \frac{3}{4} \; = \; 1\frac{1}{12}$$

Each player takes a turn. At the end of one round (one turn each), the player who has the sum closest to 1 scores a point. In case of a tie, both players score a point. After several rounds, the player with the highest score wins.

To introduce the game, demonstrate at the overhead. Write the fractions that appear on each cube, and ask the class which cube they would roll first. Roll that cube and write down your result. Ask students whether you should roll again and, if so, which cube. If you roll again, add the result to the first fraction (writing this as an equation). Continue until students suggest ending your turn. Students then find the sum. Ask a volunteer to explain or demonstrate how to add the fractions in the equation using the clock face.

Play one or two more turns for demonstration. Make sure students understand that their sum can be more than 1; they do not "bust" and lose if they go past 12:00 on the clock. Once students are clear on the rules, they play the game in groups.

Observing the Students   Observe students while they are playing. This can be a good informal assessment of students' familiarity with common fractions and their ability to add mentally. Ask students how they are deciding which cube to roll. Observe whether students seem to be learning the clock-face equivalents for different fractions, or if they always refer to their completed Student Sheet 11. Are they always finding the answers by moving game pieces around the clock face, or do they do some of the adding mentally?

Positive/Negative Scoring Variation   In a more difficult version of the game, a player's score is the *difference* between 1 and the sum of the fractions rolled. For example, a sum of $1\frac{1}{12}$ gives a score of $\frac{1}{12}$. If in the next round a player had a sum of $\frac{5}{6}$, that score would be $-\frac{1}{6}$. The combined total for the two rounds, then, would be $-\frac{1}{12}$. In this version, the winner is the one with the score closest to 0 after several rounds.

Mixed-Number Variation A version using mixed numbers can be played by including a number cube for the whole numbers 1 through 6. In this version players may, if they choose, roll the number cube along with a fraction cube. They may *not* roll the number cube alone. With the numbers rolled, they may add or subtract. Their target answer for this version is 4.

Writing Fraction Problems

Using the fraction cubes, students write at least four addition or subtraction problems, using fractions, mixed numbers, or both. They roll the cubes and use the rolled numbers to make the problems. Then they share with a partner and find the answers to both their own and their partners' problems.

Sessions 1 and 2 Follow-Up

Homework

Clock Fractions Addition Problems Students finish working on the fraction addition and subtraction problems they and their partners wrote in class. They also solve some additional fraction problems on Student Sheet 12, Clock Fractions Addition Problems. If they plan to take home a completed Student Sheet 11, Clock Fractions, to use as a reference, remind them to bring it back to school as it will continue to serve as a reference sheet throughout the unit.

Fraction Strips

What Happens

Students now work with a linear fraction model as they partition paper strips into halves, thirds, fourths, sixths, and, as a challenge, fifths. They use the strips as they look for ways that they can add two fractions together to equal a third fraction. Student work focuses on:

- partitioning paper strips into halves, thirds, fourths, and sixths
- using equivalents to partition fraction strips
- comparing fractions of different denominators
- using fraction strips to demonstrate equivalent fractions and addition of fractions

Materials

- Prepared fraction strips in five colors (1 set per student, plus extras)
- Chart paper (optional)
- Student Sheet 13 (1 per student, homework)
- Pencils
- Class list of fraction addition problems (from Sessions 1 and 2)

 Ten-Minute Math: Seeing Numbers Once or twice in the next few days, continue to do Seeing Numbers. Present the basic activity, but emphasize using fractions to describe the arrangements.

Before turning on the overhead projector, arrange a composite number of counters on the screen in a configuration that is easy to recognize. For the number 15, you might arrange 3 clumps of 5 counters. For 24, you might arrange 6 groups of 4 counters.

Show the arrangement twice for 5 seconds each time, covering it afterward. Between showings, students talk with their neighbors about what they saw.

Show the arrangement again and leave it displayed while students write and share statements and equations that describe a fraction relationship they can see in the configuration. For example:

$\frac{1}{3}$ of 15 is 5

$\frac{2}{3}$ of 15 is 10

$\frac{1}{6}$ of 24 is 4

$\frac{2}{6}$ or $\frac{1}{3}$ of 24 is 8

For complete directions and variations on this activity, see p. 124.

Teacher Checkpoint

Marking Fraction Strips

Give each student a set of fraction strips (one of each color). Have extra strips of each color available for students who make mistakes and need a new strip.

When you identify these as fraction strips, remind students of the Percent Equivalents Strips they completed, which were already partitioned into equal parts. Point out that the fraction strips are, at this point, just strips of colored paper, with nothing on them yet to show fractions. The students' challenge is to partition the strips accurately to show different fractions. Students will use these partitioned strips when they work to complete a gameboard in the next session.

List the five colors, each paired with a fraction, on the board or chart paper. Include a model showing students how to write the corresponding fraction name at the bottom of each strip. For example:

> pink—halves
>
> green—thirds
>
> blue—fourths
>
> yellow—fifths
>
> white—sixths

Mark the strips to show the different fractions. Mark one in halves, one in thirds, then one in fourths, and one in sixths. Write the marks in pencil, near the top edge. *[Illustrate by drawing a strip on the board. Label it fourths, and then mark it by eye with three tick marks along the top edge.]*

You may label the marks with fraction names if you want. Try to be as accurate as you can. Fifths are a real challenge.

When marking their strips, students write only in pencil so they can erase and move the marks if they need to. They check all five strips with their neighbors and adjust the marks until they think they are quite accurate.

Note: Avoid suggesting a particular strategy, such as folding, for deciding where to place the marks. Also do not point out relationships between halves and fourths or between halves, thirds, and sixths until students have already marked their strips. The **Teacher Note,** Students' Strategies for Partitioning Strips (p. 45), explains the reasoning for this.

As students begin working, circulate among the groups to be sure students understand the goal of making an accurately marked set of fraction strips.

You can use this activity as a checkpoint to see what your students believe about fractional parts. Observe and ask questions about the strategies students are using to place the marks and to check the placements.

■ Do they recognize that the whole strip must be preserved and that all parts must be equal?

■ Do they use equivalents to help them mark fourths and sixths?

■ What other patterns do they use? For example, do they know that the larger the denominator, the smaller the portion?

Encourage students who finish early to think of other strategies to check the accuracy of their strips. If they marked the strips by folding, encourage them to check by comparing one strip to another. Are the half marks on the halves, fourths, and sixths in the same place? Are the third marks on the thirds and sixths in the same place? If they marked the strips without folding, they can fold to check. Students who have worked in the grade 4 *Investigations* unit, *Three out of Four Like Spaghetti,* will have had experience with folding strips into halves, thirds, and fourths.

When their strips are marked, suggest they line them up, one above the other, with halves at the top and sixths at the bottom. What patterns do they see?

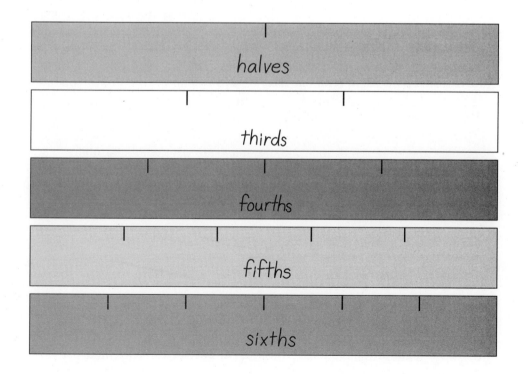

Using the Strips for Fraction Sums

Hold up a halves strip folded to show ½ and a sixths strip folded to show ⅙. Place them end to end, and compare them to the thirds strip.

I can show with fraction strips how to add some fractions. Here I have ½ and ⅙. Together they are the same length as ⅔. I can write this as an addition problem. *[Write it on the board.]*

$$\frac{1}{2} + \frac{1}{6} = \frac{2}{3}$$

What other fraction addition problems could we show with these strips? Work with a partner. Find lengths you can put together to make other lengths. Write them down as addition problems.

Observe students as they work. If students are having difficulty getting started, write ½ + ½ = 1 on the board and ask they how they can use the fraction strips to demonstrate that is true. Then suggest that they find as many other combinations as they can that add to 1. As students are ready, suggest that they do problems with mixed numbers. For example:

$$3\frac{3}{4} + 2\frac{1}{2}$$

Collect new problems to add to the class list of fraction addition problems. Students might check problems already on this list by trying them with fraction strips. You might want to start another list of fraction subtraction problems, or modify your addition list to include subtraction. Students can use their strips and some of the fraction addition problems already listed to generate subtraction problems. For example:

Let's look at a problem from our list—maybe ½ + ⅙ = ⅔. Could you use your strips and that addition problem to make up a *subtraction* problem with the same three fractions? Think about it.

If students need more clarification, demonstrate with whole numbers. Since 2 + 3 = 5, we know that 5 − 2 = 3 and 5 − 3 = 2. You might also suggest subtraction problems that use whole numbers. For example:

$$6 - 2\frac{2}{3} \qquad 2 - \frac{3}{4}$$

Session 3 Follow-Up

Homework

Fraction Strip Subtraction Problems   Students use their fraction strips to generate four or five subtraction problems on Student Sheet 13, Fraction Strip Subtraction Problems. Remind them to be sure to bring their fraction strips back to class, to use in making a gameboard in the next session.

Students' Strategies for Partitioning Strips

Teacher Note

When we first tried making fraction strips in the classroom, we asked students to mark the strips in an order that reflected relationships between denominators; that is, we encouraged them to use halves in making fourths, and to use thirds in making sixths. Unfortunately, students who did not already know about these relationships tended to mimic the teacher without understanding. To make sense of these relationships, students need to figure them out for themselves. Now we simply suggest marking the strips in order of increasing denominator. They can, of course, use the strips they have already completed to help them mark others, but we don't tell them how.

Although adults are likely to fold strips to partition them, it's best to let students decide for themselves how to do this task. One group of fifth graders we worked with never folded at all. They placed pencils across the strips and adjusted them until the spaces between them looked equal, then marked under the pencils. They compared their markings with their neighbors and adjusted if they didn't all agree.

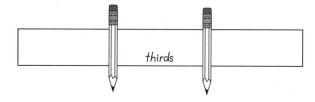

How the students approach this task depends on the knowledge of fractions they bring to it. Here are some approaches you might see in your classroom:

- **Unequal Parts** Some students think only that they must get a certain number of parts. They may just fold over and over and open up and count the parts. They will be satisfied with four parts for fourths, not caring if the parts are equal. If they fold into more parts than they are aiming for, or if it is pointed out that one part is too long, they might tear off a bit, not maintaining the original length of the whole.

- **More Shares, Smaller Shares** Other students will notice that as the denominators increase, the unit fraction becomes smaller; for example, they will know that one-fifth is a bit smaller than one-fourth. These students might estimate the length of one-fifth and then fold to copy that length across the strip, or iterate that length using their thumb or forefinger as calipers. If they get the number of portions they expected, they may not survey the whole strip to see if the last portion is smaller or larger than the others. They assume that because they used a good strategy, the portions must be equal.

- **Seeing the Whole Strip** Students who keep the strips laid flat and place markers at equal intervals along them are likely to be more accurate than either of the previous two groups. They will look at the whole strip to be sure they have the desired number of equal portions. Some will measure with a ruler to ensure that the portions are of equal length. These students often create mental images of the place of individual fractions in the whole, remembering for example that there are 2½ fifths on each side of the halfway mark.

- **Using Equivalents** Finally, some students will use equivalents to help them. Most commonly this occurs in getting fourths from halves, although these students may also use the thirds strips to mark sixths. They may use a similar strategy in Session 4 when they are marking eighths and tenths on the Fraction Track gameboard.

Don't be surprised when students have difficulty realizing that the whole must be maintained and the portions of the strips must be equal. The percent and fraction grids, the Percent Equivalents Strip, and the Fraction Clocks come to the students already partitioned into equal sections. When students do their own partitioning on the fraction strips, they need time to understand the requirements.

Session 3: Fraction Strips ■ **45**

Fraction Tracks

Materials

- Transparency of Fraction Track Gameboard, page 1
- Overhead projector and pen
- Ruler (1 per student)
- Fraction Track Gameboard, pages 1 and 2 (1 per student)
- Transparent tape
- Scissors
- Fraction Cards (1 deck per 3–4 students)
- Equivalents Chart
- Student Sheet 14 (1 per student, homework)
- Chart paper (optional)

What Happens

Students complete a set of Fraction Tracks, another linear model, showing all fractions between 0 and 1 for halves, thirds, fourths, fifths, sixths, eighths, and tenths. Students look for fraction equivalents and write about patterns they see. They count by fractions across the Fraction Track gameboard, a set of number lines from 0 to 2. Working in groups, students order fractions by size and play the game Capture Fractions. Their work focuses on:

- identifying positions of fractions between 0 and 1 on a number line
- labeling fractions on number lines
- comparing fractions with different denominators
- using equivalencies to place fractions on a set of number lines from 0 to 1
- comparing the relative size of fractions up to $3/2$

Activity

Halfway Across the Fraction Tracks

Display the transparency of page 1 of the Fraction Track Gameboard.

For this number line model, points are numbered to show their distance from 0—that is, on the thirds track, points are numbered successively from left to right, $0/3$, $1/3$, $2/3$, 1. To distinguish this from an area model that might number each portion by size (or $1/3$, $1/3$, $1/3$), introduce the labeling of the board by suggesting that a little creature is walking across each of the tracks from left to right. It stops to rest at the dots.

....

❖ **Tip for the Linguistically Diverse Classroom** Make a little sketch of this creature on the transparency. Point to its legs and use your fingers to represent walking along the track, or number line.

....

This set of fraction tracks is like your fraction strips all lined up below one another. You are going to finish marking and labeling the tracks to make a board for a fraction game. The top track shows halves, the next track shows thirds, and so on.

Suppose an ant starts at the $0/2$ [zero-halves] dot on the top track and starts walking along the line. Halfway across, the ant stops for a rest at the place labeled one-half. If this ant later starts walking across the fourths track and stops to rest halfway, where will that be?

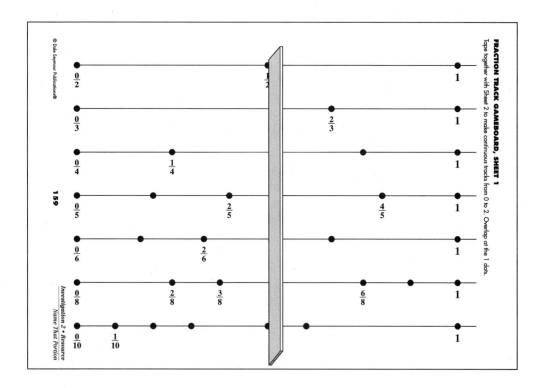

On the transparency, make a dot on the fourths track directly in line with the ½ on the halves track. To do this, demonstrate how to hold a straight-edge vertically through the ½ and (unlabeled) ⁵⁄₁₀ dots to place the dots on the midpoint of other tracks.

What should we write to label this halfway point on the fourths track?

If students suggest labeling this point ½, remind them that this is the fourths track. When you hear the name two-fourths, label the halfway dot with the fraction ²⁄₄.

What other track already has a dot at the ant's halfway stopping point?

When students identify the fraction name, write the fraction ⁵⁄₁₀ at the halfway dot on the tenths track.

What other tracks *should have* a dot for a fraction at the halfway point? How can you tell which other tracks will have dots for stopping places exactly halfway across? Which tracks will *not* have any dot halfway across? What would the label be for a dot halfway across the eighths track? What are the fraction names of the other halfway dots?

See the **Dialogue Box,** Equivalents on the Fraction Tracks (p. 52), for one class's discussion of finding equivalents to one-half.

Labeling the Fraction Tracks

With the transparency still on the overhead, distribute student copies of page 1 of the Fraction Track Gameboard. (Hold page 2 for a later activity.) Suggest that students use the transparency as a model for placing and labeling dots halfway across their tracks.

When students have marked all the halves, they work together in pairs or small groups to figure out how to continue marking and labeling their Fraction Tracks. Suggest that they work in pencil.

Be sure students realize that they have to place additional dots on the tracks before they complete the labeling. Also, watch for students putting a fraction in every row under the halfway dot—for example, writing 3/5 lined up as equivalent to 1/2. If this happens, you can simply point out that the intervals on their fifths track don't seem equal, and the students will eventually work out the inconsistency.

It's best to let students decide for themselves how to do this task. To know where to place the dots, some students may measure tracks or portions of tracks. They may notice that 1/5 and 2/5 are already marked and use the distance between them to measure and mark the dot for 3/5. Or they might use a ruler and find that the tracks are 8½ inches long, so a half is 4¼ inches and a fourth is 2⅛ inches. Some students may eyeball where dots should go, for example, marking the dot for 5/6 approximately halfway between 4/6 and 1. Some students may use equivalents to help them, especially for identifying 2/4 from 1/2, and 4/8 from 2/4, and 1/3 from 2/6.

When students have finished marking their Fraction Tracks, they work together in small groups to write about the following:

1. Equivalent fractions I can find on the tracks
2. Patterns I see in the Fraction Tracks

They can write their responses on the back of the gameboard or on notebook paper.

Patterns on the Fraction Tracks

Students have in front of them their own copies of the Fraction Track Gameboard, page 1. Ask them to share equivalent fractions they have found and patterns they see on the Fraction Tracks.

You might begin by asking what clues students used to help them place additional dots on the tracks. Then elicit observations about the general patterns on the tracks. One frequently noticed pattern is that equivalent fractions for ½ fall on those tracks with even numbers (or multiples of 2) as denominators.

Students also commonly notice that the fractions form a pattern like an arch. Students might observe that from the top of each arch, denominators increase by 1 going down both sides (as far as the sixths track), and numerators are all the same on the left side of the arches, while they increase by 1 going down the right side (as far as the sixths track). You might ask students what fractions are missing and how they would fit in with the patterns. That is, would the pattern be maintained if the gameboard included fraction tracks for sevenths and ninths? if it were extended to include elevenths and twelfths?

As students tell what equivalent fractions they have found, point these out on (or add them to) the class Equivalents chart.

Counting by Fractions

Distribute page 2 of the Fraction Track Gameboard, scissors, and transparent tape. Allow time for students to assemble their gameboards by taping page 2 to page 1. They fold back or trim off the left edge of page 2 and overlap the dots labeled with 1's to make seven continuous number lines, from 0 to 2. Tomorrow, students will use this board to play a game. Today, they become familiar with what's on it.

How are the fraction tracks on the second sheet of the gameboard the same as the tracks on the first sheet? (They both show number lines for fractions, with one denominator on each line; equivalents line up under each other.) **How are they different?** (The number lines run from 1 to 2 instead of 0 to 1; these tracks include mixed numbers.)

For practice in working with the fractions on the gameboard, suggest that students try counting by fractions across the lines of the different denominators. Start together as a group.

Let's count by halves on the halves track: ½, **1, 1½, 2.** *[Write the fractions on the board or on chart paper as you and the students recite them.]*

$\frac{1}{2}$ 1 $1\frac{1}{2}$ 2

Now let's move down to the fourths track and count by halves again, but using fourths.

You might demonstrate using a halves fraction strip to help with this. Fold the strip in half and lay it on the fourths track from 0/4 to 2/4, saying **two-fourths**; then lay it between 2/4 and 1 whole, saying **one**; move it again, saying **one and two-fourths**; move it once more and say **two**.

On what other tracks can we count by halves? (sixths, eighths, tenths) **Let's count together by halves on the sixths track.**

$$\frac{3}{6} \quad 1 \quad 1\frac{3}{6} \quad 2$$

When you think they are ready, students work in small groups, counting by halves on all the tracks with even denominators.

In your groups, try counting by thirds, fourths, and fifths on the different tracks. Work as a team, and write down each sequence of fractions you say while counting. See how many tracks you can use for each fraction you count by.

Observe students to see that they have the idea of counting by fractions across different tracks. Students from each group can then add one of their counting sequences to the board.

Activity

Ordering the Fraction Cards

For the remainder of this session and the next three sessions, students work in groups of three or four. Distribute to each group a complete set of Fraction Cards (the diamond cards from Investigation 1, plus the 38 others).

Students will be using the Fraction Cards when they play the Fraction Track Game, and the goal of this activity is to become familiar with the fractions on the cards before the game begins. In their small groups, students sort the deck of Fraction Cards, finding equivalent fractions and putting all the fractions in order by size. They might split the latter task so that one or two students order all the fractions less than 1 and the others order all the fractions greater than 1. Suggest that students challenge themselves by doing this ordering task without looking at the Fraction Track Gameboard, and refer to it only when they are stuck.

Students generally can order many of the fractions less than 1, but may need to use the Fraction Track Gameboard for ordering the fractions greater than 1. They will need to be able to equate a fraction such as 11/8 with the notation 13/8 on the gameboard.

When most groups have finished ordering their deck of Fraction Cards, ask students what equivalents they have found. Check to see if they are already on the class Equivalents chart.

Note: The numbers greater than 1 on the Fraction Cards are written not as mixed numbers but with numerators greater than denominators. In some texts, fractions greater than 1 written this way are called "improper fractions." Avoid using this term, which suggests that fractions written in this way are not "correct" as fractions, or that they should always be converted to whole or mixed numbers (as they are on the Fractions Track Gameboard). It is important that students be able to recognize and use both forms.

Capture Fractions Game

If there is time, introduce the game Capture Fractions, which is based on the card game commonly known as War. This game will be an option during Choice Time in Session 7–8, and students can play the game with family members for homework.

To play Capture Fractions, the deck of Fraction Cards (with or without the percent cards removed) is dealt out in two facedown piles, one for each player. Both players turn their top card faceup at the same time. The player who turns up the higher value takes both cards. If the cards are equivalent, players turn up another card; the player with the higher value then takes all four cards. In case of disagreements, players can refer to the Fraction Track Gameboard.

Sessions 4 and 5 Follow-Up

More In-Between   After Session 4, students continue to play the In-Between Game with their family.

Capture Fractions   After Session 5, tell students that now they will be using their home decks to teach their family more games. This time they use *all* the Fraction Cards (with or without the percent cards) to teach someone at home to play Capture Fractions. The directions are on Student Sheet 14, How to Play Capture Fractions. At the bottom of Student Sheet 14, students record the fractions turned over in two rounds, and explain how they knew which fraction was larger.

Number Lines in Use   Students look for some examples of number lines (either with fractions, with whole numbers, or with unnumbered marks) used in real life: measuring cups, speedometers, gasoline gauges, rulers, thermometers, and light-to-dark choices on copy machines. Ask students to look particularly for fractions, decimals, or marks indicating fractional parts. They make drawings of number lines they find and write about how they are used. Start a classroom display of these illustrations.

Equivalents on the Fraction Tracks

The teacher has just introduced Fraction Tracks (p. 46), and the class is looking for fractions equivalent to ½ that they could mark and label on the tracks.

My ant has hopped on down to the fourths track. Walk my ant halfway across the fourths track. Is there a dot there?

Toshi: No, but you can tell where it should be because of the ½ above it.

Can someone name it?

Desiree: I'd say two-fourths.

Does everyone agree? *[They do.]* **Why? You all dropped down and put a dot on the fourths track. Desiree gave it a name. Does someone see a relationship?**

Lindsay: Yeah. Because ½ of a 4 is a 2, and 2 plus 2 is 4.

You're telling me one-half is the same as two-fourths? *[She writes on the board.]*

$$\frac{1}{2} = \frac{2}{4}$$

Rachel: Yes. It's fifty-fifty.

Leon: They're the same.

But how do you *know* that?

Leon: Because if you shaded in … *[He draws a diagram of the halves and fourths strips on the board to show what he means.]*

Toshi: I also saw it as the one doubled and the two doubled. One and one is two, two and two is four, so two-fourths.

Can someone put my ant on another track and find another halfway point? *[The teacher circulates for a minute, checking in with students.]* **I see that some people are having trouble finding a name for one-half on the fifths track.**

Toshi: We can only do it with even numbers.

Leon: Yeah, three-sixths.

Toshi: And four-eighths.

Noah: Five-tenths.

[The teacher continues writing.]

$$\frac{1}{2} = \frac{2}{4} = \frac{3}{6} = \frac{4}{8} = \frac{5}{10}$$

One-half is the same distance as two-fourths, which is the same distance as three-sixths, which is the same distance as … *[The students join in and finish the chant, ending with five-tenths.]* **Does anyone remember the name for these? If I gave Desiree one-half of a sandwich, and I gave Rachel two-fourths of a sandwich, and Corey three-sixths of a sandwich, do you all have the same amount?**

Corey: All right! I'm getting more.

Marcus: Yes, but only in numbers.

Desiree: Breaking it up, it's the same. Three is half of six. You get half the pieces.

Here are three sandwiches. *[The teacher draws three rectangles on the board.]* **I'm giving Desiree one-half. I'm giving Rachel two-fourths. Now, we're going to divide this sandwich into sixths, and Corey, I'm giving you three of the six pieces.**

Corey: They're all equal. I thought I was going to get more, but they're the same.

Did you hear that? It's easy to fall into that trap. What happened to his pieces?

Noah: They're smaller.

So these fractions are all equal—what's another word for that?

Several students: Equivalent.

Yes, all these fractions are equivalent, but we say that ½ is the fraction expressed in lowest terms.

The Fraction Track Game

What Happens

Students play the Fraction Track Game, turning over Fraction Cards to determine their total move. As the students put together different amounts to equal the fraction turned up, they discover how fractions can be broken into parts with unlike denominators. Their work focuses on:

- finding equivalent fractions
- ordering fractions
- adding fractions
- breaking fractions into parts

 Ten-Minute Math: Seeing Numbers Once or twice in the next few days, do Seeing Numbers with your students. Try the Generating Number Sentences variation.

Show a small number of objects arranged in equal parts. To practice writing equations and other notations for computation, students working alone or in pairs generate as many number statements as they can about the arrangement. Pool all the different statements, perhaps by asking some pairs to each write one on the board. Consider, for example, an array of 24 counters in three rows of eight:

```
○ ○  ○  ○ ○ ○ ○ ○
○ ○  ○  ○  ○ ○○ ○
○ ○ ○  ○  ○○○ ○ ○
```

Possible statements include these:

$\frac{24}{8} = 3$ $\frac{1}{3}$ of 24 $= 8$ $\frac{2}{3}$ of 24 $= 16$

$\frac{1}{8}$ of 24 $= 3$ $\frac{2}{8}$ of 24 $= 6$

$24 \div 3 = 8$ $8\,\overline{)24}$

$3 \times 8 = 24$ $8 + 8 + 8 = 24$

For complete directions and variations on the Seeing Numbers activity, see p. 124.

Materials

- Chips or small counters to use as game pieces (20 per group of 3–4 students)
- Students' Fraction Track Gameboards
- Fraction Cards (1 deck per group)
- Transparency of Fraction Track Gameboard, page 1
- Student Sheet 15 (1 per student, homework)
- Overhead projector

Introducing the Fraction Track Game

Before You Begin   The Fraction Track Game is more complex than many of the other games students have been playing. The rules themselves are fairly simple, but a player's move can be enormously complex. Be sure to read the directions to the game (Student Sheet 15), read and understand the introductory example that follows, and play several games yourself before teaching the students how to play; this will help you anticipate difficulties and potential points of confusion.

Introducing the Game   Explain that there are two versions of the game. Today they will try Playing to 1, using the Fraction Tracks they completed. Later they will use the entire gameboard for Playing to 2.

Show the Fraction Track Gameboard transparency (page 1 only, with missing dots and fractions filled in) on the overhead. Place seven chips on the gameboard, one per track, on fractions less than 3/4. Show students that for this version of the game, you have removed all fractions greater than 1 from the deck of Fraction Cards, and they will need to do the same before they play.

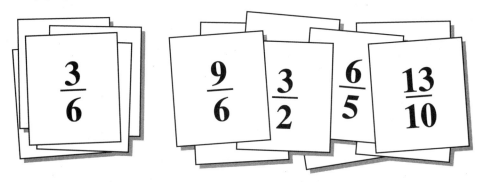

Fraction Cards   Remove all fractions greater than 1.

In this game, players take turns randomly drawing a Fraction Card and moving chips along the number lines (or *tracks*) on the gameboard for a total move equal to the fraction on the card. The chips are shared by all the players, so wherever they are left at the end of one player's turn will be the starting points for the next player's turn.

The goal is to move the chips so that one (or more) of them lands exactly on the number 1. A player may not move beyond the 1, or "wrap around" to restart the chip at the beginning of the same track during a turn. This rule is included so that players will not be able to play *only* the exact fraction on their card each time. When a chip lands on 1, if the fraction for that turn is not used up, the player must continue with a move on another track. When a chip lands on 1, the player takes that chip. A new chip is placed on the same track at 0 just before the next player's turn.

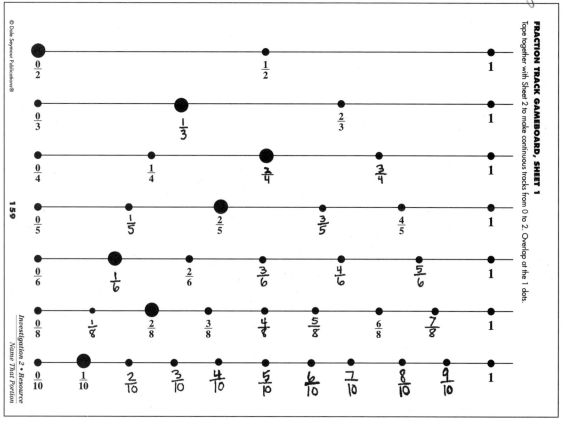

© Dale Seymour Publications®

FRACTION TRACK GAMEBOARD, SHEET 1

Tape together with Sheet 2 to make continuous tracks from 0 to 2. Overlap at the 1 dots.

$\frac{0}{2}$ $\frac{1}{2}$ 1

$\frac{0}{3}$ $\frac{1}{3}$ $\frac{2}{3}$ 1

$\frac{0}{4}$ $\frac{1}{4}$ $\frac{2}{4}$ $\frac{3}{4}$ 1

$\frac{0}{5}$ $\frac{1}{5}$ $\frac{2}{5}$ $\frac{3}{5}$ $\frac{4}{5}$ 1

$\frac{0}{6}$ $\frac{1}{6}$ $\frac{2}{6}$ $\frac{3}{6}$ $\frac{4}{6}$ $\frac{5}{6}$ 1

$\frac{0}{8}$ $\frac{1}{8}$ $\frac{2}{8}$ $\frac{3}{8}$ $\frac{4}{8}$ $\frac{5}{8}$ $\frac{6}{8}$ $\frac{7}{8}$ 1

$\frac{0}{10}$ $\frac{1}{10}$ $\frac{2}{10}$ $\frac{3}{10}$ $\frac{4}{10}$ $\frac{5}{10}$ $\frac{6}{10}$ $\frac{7}{10}$ $\frac{8}{10}$ $\frac{9}{10}$ 1

159

Investigation 2 • Resource
Name That Portion

Discuss possible moves. For example, for the board shown above, suppose you draw the ⁴/₅ card.

■ You could move ⁸/₁₀ on the tenths line (from ¹/₁₀ to ⁹/₁₀), but you would not win a chip.

■ You cannot move the whole distance on the fifths track. You could move 3 of the 4 fifths to get from ²/₅ to 1; then you must move the other fifth on another track—that is, ²/₁₀ on the tenths track.

■ Another correct (but extremely unlikely) play would be to move ¹/₂ on the fourths track (to land on 1), leaving 1¹/₂ fifths. You could move this distance on the tenths track as ³/₁₀.

Students will vary enormously in the complexity of their moves. For more examples, see the **Dialogue Box,** Playing the Fraction Track Game (p. 57).

When students play, they will take turns. For your demonstration game, draw another card as if it were someone else's turn. Move the chips on the transparency according to students' suggestions. Encourage students to think about different possible moves for the same Fraction Card and to share any strategies they are using to find them.

Playing the Fraction Track Game

Once students understand how to play the Fraction Track Game, they play in groups for the rest of the session. The game can be played by two or three players, or by pairs playing as opposing teams. Each group of players will play on one of their gameboards; they also need a deck of Fraction Cards and about 20 chips or counters. It is helpful to have several laminated gameboards available for use in the classroom.

Remind students that they need to remove the percent cards and all cards greater than 1 from the Fraction Card deck. These cards should be placed back in the envelope. Students also fold back their gameboards so that only the first half shows. You might distribute Student Sheet 15, How to Play the Fraction Track Game, if you feel it would be useful during class; students will take this sheet home as part of their homework.

Walk around and assist students as needed so they understand how to play the game. Some students will want to move only on the track that has the same denominator as the fraction on the card they picked. At times this will be impossible, as that would make them go off the end. Encourage them to think about other ways to move the same fraction by asking how they could use some or all of their fraction on another track. If they seem stuck, remind them how they used a straightedge to label equivalents. The **Dialogue Box,** Playing the Fraction Track Game (p. 57), contains excerpts from the discussions among groups playing both versions of the game, and shows when the teacher does and doesn't intervene.

When students are comfortable playing the introductory version, encourage them to try the Playing to 2 version, which uses both sheets of the gameboard and all the Fraction Cards, including those greater than 1 (but not the percent cards).

Session 6 Follow-Up

🏠 Homework

The Fraction Track Game Students take home their own Fraction Track Gameboard and Student Sheet 15, How to Play the Fraction Track Game, to teach the game to their families. They should still have the deck of Fraction Cards they took home during Investigation 1. Advise students to be patient teachers, as this game is challenging for many adults. (Keep in mind that you will continue to need completed gameboards for playing in class.)

Playing the Fraction Track Game

This teacher is observing students as they play the Fraction Track Game. The first group is engaged in the Playing to 1 version.

Sofia: I drew ⅙. *[She moves it on the sixths track.]*

Lindsay: There's not much else you can do, just half of a third, which is impossible. *[Draws a card.]* I've got ⅛. Same for me *[meaning, no choice but to move it on the eighths track]*.

Manuel: Mine's ⅖. I'll go 1... 2 tenths... no, 4 tenths.

Sofia: *[She draws 2/2.]* I've got a half here [on the halves track] for a chip, and then I'll move 5 tenths for the other half.

Lindsay: How come? Oh, right. One-half is lined up with 5/10. I get it. OK, my turn. *[Takes a card.]* I picked 4/4. A whole 1. Well, I can move 1 fourth to get a chip. Then I think I'll do 1 half, and that leaves me with 1 more fourths.

Sofia: You can't do fourths again. You can do 2 eighths.

These students are figuring out equivalents and becoming familiar with the gameboard. The teacher plans to look in on them again a bit later and encourage them to try Playing to 2.

The next group has moved on to Playing to 2. The teacher has suggested that whenever the players move on more than one track, they record their play as an equation. They are helping one another split their moves.

Noah: OK, I picked 7/10. I think I'll move 1 third. Now I have 1 third left.

Alani: ⅓ and ⅓ is 7/10? That doesn't sound right.

Noah: Let me check. *[He holds a straightedge at 7/10, perpendicular to the tracks, and ⅔ doesn't quite line up.]* Nope.

Alani: Yeah—7/10 is 70 percent, and ⅔ is 66⅔ percent, so 7/10 is more.

Jasmine: It's 7/10, right? There's 5 tenths in a half, so maybe we can start with ½.

Yu-Wei: If it's tenths, we could do fifths, too.

Noah: *[Checks the gameboard with the straightedge.]* 2/10 is ⅕.

Yu-Wei: No, ⅕ is half of a tenth, isn't it?

Noah: No, look: 1 fifth and 2/10 line up. You got it backwards. So let's move 1 fifth. Now I have 5/10 left over. That's a half, and we could move a half almost anywhere. So I'm going to do 3 sixths to get a chip. *[He records 7/10 = ⅕ + 3/6.]* You're up, Yu-Wei.

Yu-Wei: I picked 6/4. I'm going to move 1 fourth first to get to the end. *[He moves a chip from 1¾ to 2.]* Now, I'll move 6 eighths. That's equal to 3 fourths. So I have 4 fourths used up so far... and 1 half left. That's easy. I can do it anywhere... 3 sixths. Now, let's see... ¼ and 2/4 [3/6] is ¾ and another ¾ [6/8] is 6/4. *[He records 6/4 = ¼ + 6/8 + 3/6.]*

Jasmine: OK, 14/10. I'm going to move 2 tenths *[she moves the chip on the tenths track]*. Then instead of 12 tenths I can do 6 fifths, and it's a chip.

Alani: Here's 3/3. I'm going to try to start with 1 sixth 'cause I get a chip... *[pause]* I need some help.

Yu-Wei: That counts for half of ⅓. *[He shows this by using his fingers as calipers, one on the 5/6 and the other on the 1, and then moving them to the thirds track.]*

Alani: Then I'll move 4 eighths, and 4/8 is... This is hard to think about in thirds! It's 1 third and then *[using her fraction strips]* another half of a third?

Yu-Wei: Right! So put the 2 halves of the thirds together, and that's another third, so you've done ⅔, and there's ⅓ left, and you can move it on the thirds line. You got a triple! *[Writes 3/3 = ⅙ + 4/8 + ⅓.]*

Fraction Games

Materials

- Fraction Cards
- Fraction Track Gameboards
- Chips or counters (20 per group)
- Fraction cubes
- Completed Student Sheet 11 (for reference)
- Large Clock Face (optional)
- Student Sheet 16 (1 per student, homework)
- Percent Equivalents Strips (from Investigation 1)
- Class list, Everyday Uses of Fractions, Decimals, and Percents (from Investigation 1)

What Happens

During Choice Time, students play two or three of the fraction games they have already learned: the In-Between Game, Roll Around the Clock, the Fraction Track Game, and Capture Fractions. Their work focuses on:

- finding equivalent fractions and percents
- ordering fractions
- adding fractions

Choice Time: Fraction Games

Four Choices   During Sessions 7 and 8, students will have the opportunity to play the percent and fraction games they have learned in this unit. If your students are using the full-year grade 5 *Investigations* curriculum, they are already familiar with Choice Time. You might want to remind them of your particular rules—how students make and record their choices, where the materials are, and where students should work. During the two sessions, every student should play two or three of the games, but they may play them in any order they wish. Students may play with a partner or in groups of three to four. At the beginning of the session, review the directions for each game and the materials needed.

Choice 1: The In-Between Game

For the In-Between Game, students need only the diamond (♦) cards from the Fraction Cards deck. They may want to use their Percent Equivalents Strips as a reference. The game is played in pairs. Players lay out the three percent cards and take turns placing Fraction Cards in adjacent positions, keeping the numbers in order from left to right. The object is for players to place all their cards on the table. The full directions for this game are on Student Sheet 8.

Choice 2: Roll Around the Clock

For Roll Around the Clock, students use two fraction cubes (prepared earlier in Investigation 2). Use of the Large Clock Face is optional. Players may use their completed Student Sheet 11, Clock Fractions, as a reference. The game is for two to three players or two pairs playing as teams. Players roll the number cubes one at a time, with the goal of getting a sum close to 1. Or, they may play the Mixed-Number Variation, using a number cube with whole numbers as well as the fraction cubes, and adding or subtracting with the goal of getting close to 4. For complete directions to this game and its variations, see p. 38.

Choice 3: The Fraction Track Game

If your students have been successful with the Playing to 1 version of this game, discuss how to advance to the Playing to 2 version. For either version, each group will need a Fraction Track Gameboard, a deck of Fraction Cards (with percent cards removed), and about 20 chips or counters. The game can be played by two or three players, or two pairs playing as teams. For complete directions, refer to Student Sheet 15, How to Play the Fraction Track Game.

Students are likely to need guidance while playing the Fraction Track Game, as it is the most complex. You might invite a few students to play it with you, or ask students who are comfortable with the game to help others.

Choice 4: Capture Fractions

Students use a complete deck of Fraction Cards (with or without percent cards removed) to play Capture Fractions, a two-player game similar to the card game War. Cards are dealt facedown in two piles. The top card of each pile is turned up, and the player with the higher value captures both cards. See p. 51 for full directions. Students might supplement the Fraction Cards with grids saved from Investigation 1, showing different fractional amounts colored in.

Observing the Students

Once students are involved in playing the games, circulate to see how they are thinking about the math.

- Are students making use of equivalent fractions and percents?
- Are they building a repertoire of fraction addition facts?

The In-Between Game

- Do students know and use some percent equivalents to help them order the fractions?
- Can they sort fractions into those greater than and those less than ½?

Roll Around the Clock

- Can students comfortably use the clock model to add fractions?
- Can they comfortably find fraction sums above 1?

Fraction Track Game

- Do students recognize equivalents so that they can move on a track with a denominator different from that of the card they picked? For example, if they pick a card in the fifths, do they know they can also move on the tenths track?
- Can students break fractions into familiar units such as halves and wholes? For example, do they recognize that 3/4 = 1/4 + 1/2, or that 7/5 take away 5/5 (1 whole) leaves 2/5?
- After they remove the most familiar parts (the halves and wholes), can they recognize what's left? For example, do they know that 10/6 take away 6/6 (1 whole) leaves 4/6, and 4/6 take away 1/2 (3/6) leaves 1/6?

Capture Fractions

- Are students using ½ and 1 as landmarks? If they are, you may hear this sort of reasoning:

  3/5 is bigger than 1/3 because 1/3 is smaller than a half and 3/5 is bigger.

  5/6 is bigger than 3/4 because they're both missing one piece and sixths are smaller, so 5/6 is closer.

Sessions 7 and 8 Follow-Up

More Everyday Uses of Fractions, Decimals, and Percents   Call attention to the class lists of Everyday Uses of Fractions, Decimals, and Percents, started in Investigation 1. Challenge students to each bring in at least two more examples, looking particularly for decimals. They might check the newspaper, watch for them on TV, and look on packages of food or other products. They record each example they find on Student Sheet 16, More Everyday Uses of Fractions, Decimals, and Percents, and, if they are able, write brief explanations of the meaning of the decimals using equivalent (or nearly equivalent) fractions.

Making Moves on Two and Three Tracks   As students continue to play the Fraction Track Game, start a list of plays they make that use fractions on two, three, or more tracks. Students write the fraction that was on the card turned up and the moves they made on the gameboard, writing them as addition problems. For example:

$$\frac{7}{8} = \frac{1}{2} + \frac{3}{8}$$
$$\frac{3}{4} = \frac{2}{8} + \frac{1}{6} + \frac{1}{3}$$

Problems with Fractions

Materials

- Student Sheet 17 (1 per student)
- Previous fraction work for reference
- Student Sheet 18 (1 per student, homework)

What Happens

Students solve word problems using fractions and percents and later share their solution strategies. Their work focuses on:

- finding percents and fractional parts of whole numbers
- computing with fractions
- making sense of and solving word problems
- comparing fractions

Activity

Fractions of Pizza

Students work individually on Student Sheet 17, Fractions of Pizza. In solving these problems, students use whatever materials and illustrations they find helpful. They can refer to materials in their folders as needed. Emphasize making sense of the particular problems, rather than finding a way to use the fraction models introduced earlier. For example, students may well find drawing pizzas to be more helpful than using grids or strips.

❖ **Tip for the Linguistically Diverse Classroom**   Pair students who have limited English proficiency with those who read easily, for reading aloud each problem as needed. As necessary, students can add sketches to the sheet to help with unfamiliar vocabulary.

Observing the Students   Circulate while students are working and observe how they are thinking about the problems. If students are using a conventional algorithm, ask them to explain why it works and challenge them to find another solution as well. Following are the answers, along with some questions and issues to consider as you evaluate student work:

- **Problem 1 answer:** 9 pizzas.

  Consider: This is a multiplication problem, but students are not expected to recognize it as such. Check to see how students go about solving this problem. Do they draw a picture to help? Do they see that the "leftover" fourths of three pizzas will serve another child?

- **Problem 2 answers: (a)** 1/2, 50% **(b)** 3/8, 37 1/2% **(c)** 4/10, 40% **(d)** Alyssa ate the most and Bianca ate the least.

  Consider: Can students record the information in this problem as a fraction and find the equivalent percent? Do they use the percents they found in questions (a) through (c) to answer (d)?

- **Problem 3 answer:** They both ate the same.

  Consider: Do students add the fractions in an order that is helpful? For example, 1/2 + 1/4 = 3/4, and 2/8 of the 3/8 added to that makes 1 whole, with 1/8 more, so Tito ate 1 1/8 pizzas. What other strategies do they use? Do any students compare without adding?

- **Problem 4 answers: (a)** 1/4 **(b)** Sanctora got $9, her brother $3.

  Consider: Are students able to find 3/4 of $12? Do students find 1/4 or 2/4 (1/2) first, to help them find 3/4?

- **Problem 5 answers: (a)** 75% **(b)** 375 students

  Consider: Students may not recognize 500 as a number that is divisible by 4. Do they use landmarks or familiar numbers to solve this problem? For example, they might say that 25 percent (or one-fourth) of 400 is 100, and 25 percent of 100 is 25, so the total of adults is 125. What other strategies do they use?

- **Problem 6 answer:** We ate 3 5/8 pizzas. Each person ate about 3/8 of a pizza.

  Consider: How do students subtract a mixed number from a whole number? A useful strategy is to subtract the whole number first, then the fraction: 5 – 1 = 4, and 4 – 3/8 = 3 5/8. Can students then reason out how much pizza each person ate? Here's one approach: If the 10 people had eaten all 5 pizzas, they would have each eaten half, or 4/8. Since there were 1 3/8 pizzas left (or 11 pieces), each person ate about 1/8 less than half, or about 3/8 pizza.

When everyone has finished, discuss the problems and students' strategies for finding solutions. Especially look for multiple solutions to problem 3, adding fractions of pizza.

Session 9 Follow-Up

Homework

Moves on the Fraction Track Students continue playing the Fraction Track Game with their families. They record moves they made using more than one track on Student Sheet 18, Moves on the Fraction Track.

INVESTIGATION 3

Exploring Decimals

What Happens

Session 1: Interpreting Decimals Students discuss common uses of decimals. Using a calculator, they find several division problems that have answers of 0.5, 0.25, 0.75, and other familiar decimals. To explore one application of decimals, they choose sports teams to follow over the next two weeks, keeping track of win/loss records and predicting changes in the "percentage" of games won.

Session 2: Decimals on Grids Using a model familiar from fraction and percent activities, students represent tenths and hundredths on grids. They then play a decimal game, Fill Two, which involves combining decimals on grids.

Sessions 3 and 4: Decimal Games During Choice Time, students play three decimal games that involve ordering decimal numbers expressed in tenths, hundredths, and thousandths: Smaller to Larger, Decimals In-Between, and Capture Decimals. They also continue to play Fill Two and its variation Fill Four, combining decimals to fill 10-by-10 grids.

Sessions 5 and 6: Fractions to Decimals Students find decimals of up to three digits that have a value between that of two given decimals. Students then find decimal equivalents for fractions on the calculator, making a Fraction to Decimal Division Table for all fractions with numerators and denominators from 1 to 12. They identify and explain patterns within the table.

Session 7: Fraction, Percent, and Decimal Problems Students solve word problems involving fraction, decimals, and percents, and share their strategies. They also discuss any changes in the ranking of the sports teams they have been following.

Session 8: Comparing Fractional Amounts In an assessment activity that draws on students' experiences in the first three investigations, small groups make posters that show many ways to compare two fractional amounts. They may use any notations or models they find useful to support their arguments.

Mathematical Emphasis

- representing decimals on grids
- reading and writing decimals
- ordering decimals
- dividing to find decimal equivalents of fractions
- adding decimals on a grid
- comparing fractions using different models and notations
- making sense of and solving word problems

What to Plan Ahead of Time

Materials

- Class list from Investigations 1 and 2, Everyday Uses of Decimals (Session 1)
- Sports section of any newspaper (Session 1)
- Calculators: 1 per student (Sessions 1, 5–8)
- Crayons or colored markers: assorted colors to share (Sessions 2–4, 8)
- Overhead projector, overhead pens, blank transparency (Sessions 2–6)
- Large paper, white or colored, for posters: 1 sheet per small group (Session 8)

Other Preparation

- Duplicate student sheets and teaching resources (located at the end of this unit) in the following quantities. If you have Student Activity Booklets, copy only the items marked with an asterisk.

For Session 2

Student Sheet 19, How to Play Fill Two (p. 161): 1 per student (homework)

Decimal Grids (p. 168): 3 transparencies,* 1 per small group (optional), and 1 per student (homework)

Decimal Cards, Set A (p. 169): 1 per pair (on card stock) and 1 per student (homework)

Grids (p. 178): 4–6 sheets per student, and 2 transparencies*

For Sessions 3–4

Student Sheet 20, How to Play Smaller to Larger (p. 162): 1 per student

Decimal Grids (p. 168): 1 per student (homework)

Decimal Cards, Sets A and B (p. 169): 1 deck per pair (on card stock), and 1 deck of Set B per student (homework)

Grids (p. 178): 3–4 sheets per student, (class); 3–4 sheets per student (homework)

For Sessions 5–6

Student Sheet 21, Fraction to Decimal Division Table (p. 163): 1 per student, and 1 transparency*

Student Sheet 22, Fraction, Decimal, Percent Equivalents (p. 164): 1 per student (homework)

For Session 7

Student Sheet 23, Scoring Sports and Other Problems (p. 165): 1 per student

Student Sheet 24, Comparing Common Fractions (p. 166): 1 per student (homework)

For Session 8

Student Sheet 25, More Fraction Comparisons (p. 167): 1 per student (homework)

- On a blank transparency or sheet of paper, draw a blank square the same size as each grid on the Decimal Grids sheet (p. 168)
- For Sessions 3 and 4, label 3 small squares of paper or index cards with the fractions $\frac{1}{10}$, $\frac{1}{2}$, and $\frac{9}{10}$ for each pair of students.
- Have a small supply of the following for students to use in Session 8: Clock Fractions (p. 149); Decimal Grids (p. 168); Grids (p. 178); fraction strips (in five colors, as prepared for Investigation 1)
- Cut apart the two sheets of Decimal Cards that you duplicated on card stock and store each deck in an envelope or resealable plastic bag. Use paper clips or rubber bands to separate Set A and Set B.

Interpreting Decimals

What Happens

Students discuss common uses of decimals. Using a calculator, they find several division problems that have answers of 0.5, 0.25, 0.75, and other familiar decimals. To explore one application of decimals, they choose sports teams to follow over the next two weeks, keeping track of win/loss records and predicting changes in the "percentage" of games won. Student work focuses on:

- interpreting common uses of decimals
- finding equivalent fractions and decimals

Materials

- Class list, Everyday Uses of Decimals
- Newspaper sports sections
- Calculators (1 per student)

Activity

Interpreting Decimals

Return to the list started in Investigation 1, Everyday Uses of Decimals. Collect additional examples from students and add them to the list. If they have not found a variety of uses, add a few of your own. For example:

> Rainfall in the last 24 hours: 0.25 inch
> Total rain for the month: 5.43 inches
> Car odometer: 47364.3 miles
> Baseball player's batting average: .346
> Swimmer's time in 50-meter freestyle: 30.85 seconds
> Winning cyclist's average speed: 23.51 mph

Allow a few minutes for students to read each decimal number and decide with their neighbors what it means. As they discuss the examples on your list, listen to see what they understand about decimals. Do they, for example, recognize that 0.25 inch is ¼ inch, or that 5.43 inches is almost 5½ inches? Do they understand that 0.3 mile is different from 0.3 yard? Do they recognize that 0.85 second is less than 1 second, and as such is beyond what most everyday clocks and watches can measure?

Students who follow baseball may know that a batting average of .346 is very good, but be unable to provide further explanation. Some may be able to explain batting averages and how they are calculated (number of hits divided by number of times at bat) and will be familiar with the range from poor to very good batting averages.

If money is not included on the class list, add it, writing an amount such as $285.49. Ask students to relate the decimals in money to decimals used in other situations.

How is the decimal in $285.49 similar to the decimals in the other examples? How is the "point 49" part less than 1?

Students are likely to think of "point 49" as 49 cents—a whole number of cents—rather than as 49 hundredths of a dollar. Help them recognize the decimal meaning of a cent as one-hundredth of a dollar and $.49 as ⁴⁹/₁₀₀ of a dollar, or 49 out of 100 parts of a dollar.

Fractions to Decimals on the Calculator

Write on the board:

    0.5   0.25

How would you read these decimals?

Some students may read the decimals as "point five" and "point two five." Such a reading is not incorrect, but you may want to point out that the connection between fractions and decimals will be clearer if they read a one-place decimal as *tenths* (0.5 = ⁵/₁₀) and a two-place decimal as *hundredths* (0.25 = ²⁵/₁₀₀). Five-tenths is a name of one-half because 5 is half of 10. Twenty-five hundredths is one-fourth because 25 is one-fourth of 100. Students will have more experiences reading decimals in tenths, hundredths, and thousandths over the next few sessions.

What familiar fractions are these decimals equal to?

As students suggest the equivalents, add them to the board:

    $0.5 = \frac{1}{2}$ $0.25 = \frac{1}{4}$

If fractions and decimals are two ways of writing the same thing, why do you think we need both forms?

Here's one reason: Sometimes, especially when we are computing, decimals are easier to work with. Fractions may have all kinds of different denominators—thirds, sevenths, twelfths—and it can get pretty complicated trying to compute with them. Decimals are easier because they are always expressed in multiples of 10—tenths, hundredths, thousandths, and so on.

Erase the 0.5 and 0.25, leaving the fractions ½ and ¼ on the board.

Now, suppose I wanted to express these fractions as decimals, but I didn't know how. Who knows how I could use a calculator to find out? Try it.

As necessary, remind students that a fraction is another form of division notation, so that any fraction can be thought of as a division problem. The line between the numbers is like a division sign: ½ represents 1 divided by 2 (1 divided into two parts), and ¼ represents 1 divided by 4. Doing the division on the calculator gives us the decimal equivalent on the display.

Next, challenge students to find several other ways to get these same decimals on a calculator, using different division problems.

When we divide 1 by 2 on the calculator, we get 0.5 on the display. What other numbers could you divide to get 0.5?

Write 0.5 on the board, and list division problems that students suggest. Write them both with a division sign and as fractions. As a challenge, you might give them *part* of another problem, such as 50 ÷ ?

0.5	
1 ÷ 2	$\frac{1}{2}$
2 ÷ 4	$\frac{2}{4}$
3 ÷ 6	$\frac{3}{6}$
50 ÷ ?	$\frac{50}{?}$

Explain that students will be making similar lists for some other decimals they have seen. Write 0.25 and a few other decimals that you think will be familiar to students, such as 0.75, 0.1 and 2.5. Students take a moment to think and to talk with their neighbors about what fractions these decimals are equivalent to. They then search with a calculator for three or four division problems that result in each decimal, keeping a list for each one.

While students are getting started, visit those who seem to be having difficulty. Suggest some problems that will give answers of 0.5 and 0.25 for them to write down and enter on the calculator. Once they try these, challenge them to find other problems that will give the same answers.

If students can't think of more than one fraction for each problem, suggest beginnings of problems (the numerators), perhaps as a sharing problem. For example, for 0.1, students are likely to find 1 ÷ 10 or ⅒. You could suggest another possible problem with this situation:

I had 4 pizzas at my party. Each person got 1 tenth of a pizza. How many people were there?

Write this as 4 ÷ ? = 0.1; students can then explore this on their calculator.

As students finish their lists, ask volunteers to write one or two division problems on the board under the appropriate decimal.

Win/Loss Records

Look in the sports section of your local paper to find win/loss statistics for any team sport currently being reported. You might find, for example, something like the following baseball statistics. Try to choose some that include one record of .500. Write the records on the board in table form, showing for each team the number of wins, number of losses, and the corresponding "percentage" of wins (expressed as a decimal).

American League, East Division

	W	L	Pct.
Boston	11	5	.688
New York	10	7	.588
Toronto	9	9	.500
Detroit	7	10	.412
Baltimore	6	10	.375

You found many uses of decimals on the sports pages. Here's a common one, used in comparing the standings of different teams. Look in the last column. Does anyone know what these decimals mean?

Some students may be quite sophisticated in their understanding of the figures; others will have never seen them before. Establish the fact that W represents the number of games a team has won, and L is the number of games lost. The decimal number is the *number* of games won out of the total played. This number is especially useful when we are trying to compare teams whose records seem very close, but because they haven't played exactly the same number of games, it's hard to tell which team has a better record. It may be helpful to add a column for total games played by each team.

Point out that the numbers indicating *percentage* are not in conventional form with % signs, but reported as three-place decimals.

Suppose these were written with the percent (%) sign. What percent does .500 represent? How do you know? What sort of win/loss record gives you .500?

Students may recognize .500 as equal to 50% and see that it means a team has won exactly half (50 percent) of its games.

Write on the board:

$$\frac{\text{number of games won}}{\text{number of games played}}$$

Ask a volunteer to come to the board to write the fraction used to find the win/loss percentage of .500:

$\frac{9}{18}$ $9 \div 18 = 0.5$ which is equivalent to .500

Briefly discuss what the other percentages in the table mean—that the higher the decimal, the greater number of games won out of the total games played. Allow a little time for students to experiment with a calculator to see if they can determine the fractions and obtain the percentages listed for the other teams. While this procedure may make sense to some students, others may be quite confused. Keep in mind that the purpose is not to make students proficient in calculating win/loss percentages, but for them to see decimals used in a real situation and to have some general understanding of what the numbers mean.

Tell students that for the next two weeks, they are going to choose some sports teams and keep track of their win/loss records. (The sport chosen will vary with the time of year.) This can be done as a group activity in class, or as an individual activity for ongoing homework. If you do it as a whole group, set up a table for each team on chart paper; otherwise, individual students set up their own tables on notebook paper, as follows:

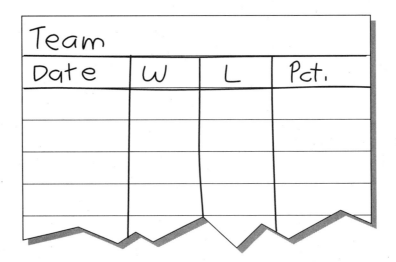

Students start by entering each team's current record using data from the sports section you have in class. After each subsequent game, students change the win/loss data to reflect the game's result. They try to predict the new percentage before checking in the newspaper or with a calculator. If they follow all the teams in a particular league or division, students can track how the rankings change from week to week.

Session 1 Follow-Up

Extensions

Weekly Rainfall Many newspapers, in the weather section, report rainfall records for different parts of the country. They list amounts each day and for the month and year to date, in hundredths of an inch. Students might pick a city and keep track of its rainfall each day for a week. At the end of the week, students total the rainfall and enter the data for each city on a class chart. Students then use this data to write problems comparing the rainfall in different cities.

Percentage of Fats in Foods Most food packages provide information about the nutritional content of a single serving. They show the total calories in a serving, and the fat calories in a serving. For example, a box of snack crackers indicates it this way:

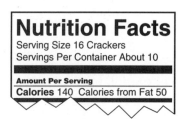

Nutrition Facts
Serving Size 16 Crackers
Servings Per Container About 10

Amount Per Serving
Calories 140 Calories from Fat 50

Students could use this information and a calculator to investigate the percentage of fat in various foodstuffs. They would divide the fat calories by the total calories and write the answer as a percent. So, for example, the percent of fat in the snack crackers would be $50/140 = 0.357 = 35.7\%$. The class might then pick categories and list foods according to their fat content; for example:

Not too fatty	A little fatty	Very fatty	Almost all fat
<10%	10–30%	30–90%	>90%

Many groups concerned about keeping Americans healthy suggest having a diet less than 30% fat; some suggest much less.

Decimals on Grids

Materials

- Blank square (same size as each grid on the Decimal Grids sheet)
- Decimal Grids transparency (3 copies)
- Decimal Grids (1 per small group, optional, and 1 per student, homework)
- Grids (4–6 sheets per student)
- Grids transparency (2 copies)
- Decimal Cards, Set A (1 per pair and 1 per student, homework)
- Student Sheet 19 (1 per student, homework)
- Overhead projector and pens
- Crayons or colored markers to share

What Happens

Using a model familiar from fraction and percent activities, students represent tenths and hundredths on grids. They then play a decimal game, Fill Two, which involves combining decimals on a grid. Student work focuses on:

- representing decimals on grids
- reading and writing decimals
- ordering decimals
- adding decimals on a grid

 Ten-Minute Math: Exploring Data Once or twice in the next few days, during any free 10 minutes, do the Exploring Data activity with your students. Choose a question that involves data that students know or can easily observe; for example:

What color shirt [or sweater, or other top] are you wearing today?

Quickly collect and display the data using a table, a line plot, or a bar graph. Ask students to describe the data. Encourage students to use fractions when describing data; for example:

5 out of the 24 students, or 5 twenty-fourths, are wearing blue.

12 out of 24 students, or one-half, are wearing white or almost white shirts.

Save all the data that you collect during these Ten-Minute Math activities for student use in making circle graphs in Investigation 4.

For complete directions and variation on this activity, see p. 126.

Decimals on Grids

Show students the blank square you have prepared, either on the overhead or on a sheet of paper. Explain that this is one whole. Place a transparency of Decimal Grids on the overhead projector. If the grids appear too small, gather the students together close to the screen. Or distribute copies of Decimal Grids for students to look at in small groups.

These grids are similar to those you used to show fractions and percents, but these show how one whole can be divided into decimals. How are the four grids different?

Allow students time to figure out and discuss the number of parts in each grid. The first grid is divided into 10 equal parts, the second into 100, the third into 1000, and the fourth into 10,000.

Write 0.1 on the board or overhead. Ask for volunteers to come to the overhead and color in one-tenth on each of the grids.

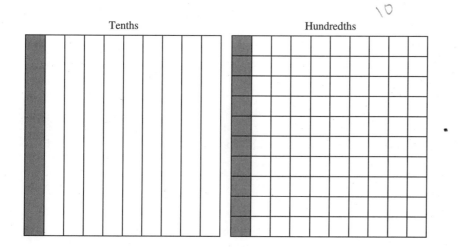

Tenths

Hundredths

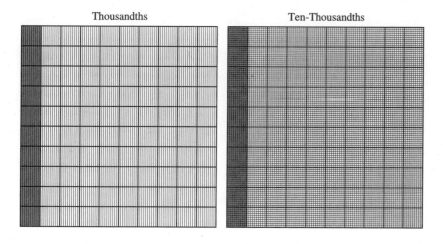

Thousandths

Ten-Thousandths

Which of these grids most clearly shows one-tenth?

Look at the way one-tenth is colored on the other three grids. From this, try to figure out how we would write one-tenth as hundredths, as thousandths, and as ten-thousandths. For each grid, write it both as a decimal and a fraction.

Students discuss the question in small groups, write down their answers, and then share responses. Record their answers on the transparency or on the board in the following way:

$$0.1 \ = \ \frac{1}{10} \quad \text{1 tenth}$$

$$0.10 \ = \ \frac{10}{100} \quad \text{10 hundredths}$$

$$0.100 \ = \ \frac{100}{1000} \quad \text{100 thousandths}$$

$$0.1000 = \frac{1000}{10,000} \quad \text{1000 ten-thousandths}$$

One-tenth is equal to 1000 ten-thousandths. [*Write on the board:* 0.1 = 0.1000] **How can you convince each other that these decimals and fractions are all equal?**

Allow time for students to explain their thoughts and reasoning to each other. Encourage them to refer to the amounts colored in on the grids. Circulate to hear their explanations.

Using a clean Decimal Grids transparency, follow a similar procedure to show hundredths with 0.75; then use a third transparency to show thousandths with 0.125. First write a decimal, asking students to read the amount. Volunteers then color in that amount on each grid on the transparency. Discuss how the amount could be written both as a decimal and a fraction to represent the amount colored in each grid.

Students may have difficulty coloring 0.75 on the tenths grid and writing it as a fraction. If so, have the other grids colored in first, and then discuss with the class how to color it on the tenths grid.

Students also might have difficulty representing this colored-in grid with a decimal and a fraction. You might point out that it's fine to write a fraction within a fraction, for seven and one-half tenths:

$$\frac{7\frac{1}{2}}{10}$$

However, it is not conventional to include a fraction with decimals (0.7½); the extra half of a tenth is generally represented as five hundredths (0.7<u>5</u>). A similar situation arises with 0.125; there is no conventional way to express this amount in only one or two decimal places, although the amount is easy to color on all the grids.

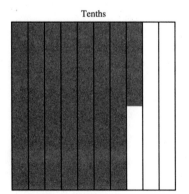

Tenths

0.75

Fill Two

Distribute a sheet of Grids to each student and place a Grids transparency on the overhead. Explain that these sheets will be used in a decimal game the students are going to play. Today they will play the game using only tenths and hundredths. Later they will also play the game using thousandths.

Write 0.25 and 0.3 on the board.

Which of these two decimals is greater? How do you know?

Invite students to use the grids on the overhead to illustrate their explanations. Some students may find it helpful to express the decimals as fractions.

Next write 0.05, 0.5, and 0.50 on the board.

What's the difference between these three decimals? Which is worth the least? How do you know?

Encourage students to discuss this in small groups. Suggest they write the decimals as fractions and show them on the grids. The **Dialogue Box,** Ordering Decimals (p. 77), has a discussion that took place in one classroom.

Introducing Fill Two   Before introducing the game Fill Two, you should have read the complete directions on Student Sheet 19 and tried playing the game yourself. You might teach the game by having two students model it on the overhead, using a Grids transparency and the Decimal Cards, Set A. During the demonstration, one student can use the top two grids and the other can use the bottom two.

To begin the demonstration game, mix up the Decimal Cards and turn over four cards. Record the amounts on the board so all students can see. Each player, in turn, chooses one of the four cards, colors in the amount on a grid on the transparency, and writes the decimal below the grid. Remember that a decimal may not be split between two grids. For example, if the card chosen is 0.75, a player cannot color in 0.5 on one grid and 0.25 on another; the whole amount must be colored in on only one grid.

After each turn, replace the card that was chosen with another card from the deck so a player always has four cards to select from. At the end of the game (when no more can be colored on the grids), the players write as an equation the amount colored in on each of their grids. For example, one grid might be 0.45 + 0.1 + 0.35 = 0.9 and the other 0.85 = 0.85 only.

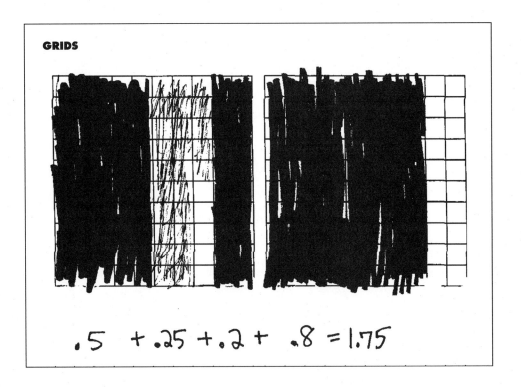

GRIDS

$$.5 + .25 + .2 + .8 = 1.75$$

Playing Fill Two Students play the game in pairs for the remainder of the session. Give each pair the Decimal Cards, Set A. Pairs can keep their decks in an envelope or resealable plastic bag labeled with both their names; they should also label the back of every decimal card with their initials, lightly in pencil. Be sure to distribute only Set A at this time; Set B (Thousandths) will be added to the deck in Session 3.

Some students may find it helpful to write the percent equivalents on all the Decimal Cards. If they choose to do this, suggest that they use pencil and write lightly.

Make available copies of the Grids sheet. Students need crayons or markers in two colors. Encourage players to use each copy of the Grids sheet for two games of Fill Two, coloring in the top two grids for their first game and the bottom two grids for a second game. Remind students to record below the grid each decimal they color in, and to form addition equations with these numbers to find the totals at the end of the game.

Session 2 Follow-Up

 **Homework**

Fill Two Students play Fill Two with their families. The class sets of Decimal Cards should remain in class, so send home another copy of the Decimal Cards, Set A, with each student, along with several copies of the Grids sheet, a copy of Student Sheet 19, How to Play Fill Two, and a copy of Decimal Grids for reference. Advise students to keep the Decimal Cards in a safe place at home for use later in this unit.

Ordering Decimals

Students are often confused about which zeros in decimals change their value. The teacher in this class walked around as students discussed the difference between 0.5, 0.05, and 0.50. At one table, the teacher heard the following reasoning.

Shakita: I don't see the difference between 0.5, 0.05, and 0.50.

Tai: They're all half of something, aren't they?

Cara: Let's write them as fractions. The first one is tenths, and the other two are both hundredths. I don't remember which zero we can leave off. *[She writes the three as fractions.]*

$$\frac{5}{10} \qquad \frac{05}{100} \qquad \frac{50}{100}$$

Antonio: It's like the remote on the TV. You can punch in zero five for channel five.

Cara: Then $^{05}/_{100}$ is the same as $^{5}/_{100}$.

Tai: And 0.5 and 0.50 are both halves—5 out of 10, and 50 out of 100.

Shakita: There's no card in the deck that has 0.50 on it.

Tai: Because it's equal to 0.5—remember, there are no cards that are equal in the deck.

Shakita: So 0.05 is a lot smaller than 0.5 because 5 hundredths is much less than 50 hundredths.

Decimal Games

Materials

- Overhead projector, pens, blank transparency

- Decimal Cards, Sets A and B (1 deck per pair)

- Decimal Cards, Set B (1 deck per student, homework)

- Grids (3–4 sheets per student, class; 3–4 sheets per student, homework)

- Colored markers or crayons to share

- Student Sheet 20 (1 per student)

- Decimal Grids (1 per student, homework)

- Prepared squares of paper or index cards (3 per pair)

What Happens

During Choice Time, students play three decimal games that involve ordering decimal numbers expressed in tenths, hundredths, and thousandths: Smaller to Larger, Decimals In-Between, and Capture Decimals. They also continue to play Fill Two and its variation, Fill Four, combining decimals to fill 10-by-10 grids. Their work focuses on:

- reading and writing decimals
- ordering decimals
- adding decimals

Activity

Smaller to Larger Game

At the beginning of Session 3, teach the Smaller to Larger Game. Before teaching the game, be sure you have tried playing it yourself. The complete set of directions is on Student Sheet 20, How to Play Smaller to Larger.

You may want to teach this game by demonstrating a collaborative solitaire version on the overhead. On a blank transparency, draw a 3-by-3 game mat, like a large tic-tac-toe grid. Explain to the students that usually two, three, or four of them will play the game together, each with their own game mat, but the game can also be played by one person, or collaboratively with several people planning together how to fill one game mat.

The object of the game is for each player to fill all the spaces on the mat with decimals from the full deck of Decimal Cards (Set A and Set B). The numbers must be placed in increasing order from left to right in each row, and in increasing order from top to bottom in each column. Once a card is placed on the game mat, it cannot be moved.

For the demonstration game, draw cards from the deck one at a time and decide, as a class, where to put each one. Instead of actually placing the cards on the mat as students will do when they play, you will need to write in the decimals in the spaces on the transparency (or, you could prepare a transparent deck of Decimal Cards for this demonstration).

Distribute a copy of Student Sheet 20, How to Play Smaller to Larger, to each student. Briefly go over the rules. Be sure students understand that the game mat they draw must be large enough to fit Decimal Cards in the spaces.

Everyone plays the game once before starting Choice Time. If students are unsure which of two numbers is larger, or if members of the group are not able to agree, encourage them to shade in grids for the numbers in question.

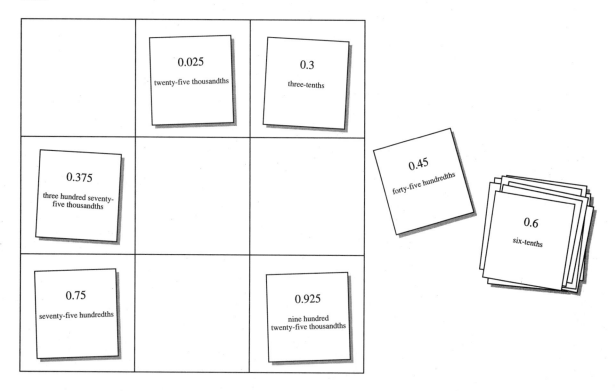

Choice Time: Decimal Games

Four Choices For the rest of this session and during the next session, students play four decimal games: Smaller to Larger, Fill Two or Fill Four (a more advanced variation), Decimals In-Between (a decimal version of Fractions In-Between), and Capture Decimals (a decimal version of Capture Fractions). Students may choose to play only with Set A (tenths and hundredths) or they may use the full deck of Decimal Cards in each game, including the thousandths (Set B). Students may choose to play two, three, or all four of the games.

If you haven't already done, distribute the Decimal Cards, Set B, to each pair of students. Students write their initials lightly on the back of each card and add these to their Decimal Cards, Set A (from Session 2). Briefly introduce the games students haven't yet played, reminding them of the fraction versions they played during Investigation 2.

Choice 1: Smaller to Larger

Students play in groups of two to four. Remind students that each player makes his or her own game mat to fill in.

Choice 2: Fill Two or Fill Four

Explain Fill Four, the variation of the game Fill Two. Student Sheet 19, How to Play Fill Two, provides the complete set of directions for both games. To play Fill Four, players fill in all four grids on a Grids sheet.

Remind students that all players use their own Grids sheet for each game. Also remind them to write the decimal below the grid each time they color in a decimal, and to write an equation at the end of the game that tells the total amount colored on all four grids.

Choice 3: Decimals In-Between

For Decimals In-Between, each pair needs three small squares of paper or index cards labeled with the fractions $\frac{1}{10}$, $\frac{1}{2}$, and $\frac{9}{10}$.

The rules to this game are the same as on Student Sheet 8, How to Play the In-Between Game, except that this game uses Decimal Cards instead of the Fraction Cards, and the three fractions (above) replace the three percents (10%, 50%, and 90%). Also, note that three decimals (0.05, 0.025, and 0.075) can be played to the left of $\frac{1}{10}$, and three (0.95, 0.925, 0.975) can be played to the right of $\frac{9}{10}$. Before students play the game, have them look through the deck to identify these six special cards. Review the rules with students as you explain how this variation differs from the original game.

Playing this game with the full set of Decimal Cards requires that students consider the order of decimals expressed as tenths, hundredths, and thousandths. If the game is too difficult for some of your students, they might play it with just three or four cards per player. Students could also play a noncompetitive version of the game by drawing four to six cards and collaborating to put these in order.

Make available copies of Grids that can be shaded when students need help in ordering the decimals. If students find it helpful to write the decimals as fractions in order to compare them, remind them to refer to the decimal names written on the cards.

Choice 4: Capture Decimals

Capture Decimals is played by pairs. The deck of Decimal Cards is dealt out into two facedown piles, one for each player. Both players turn their top card faceup at the same time. The player who turns up the highest value takes both cards and puts them aside. As in the other two games, encourage students to use Grids or to try writing the decimals as fractions when they need help comparing the value of two decimals.

Choice Time provides an opportunity for you to circulate and observe your students as they interpret decimals while they play games. Below are some things to look for as you circulate.

Smaller to Larger

- Do students understand and follow the rules for placing cards—that each row (from left to right) and each column (from top to bottom) increases? Do players check each other's card placement?

- How do students order decimals? Do they, for example, recognize that 0.35 is greater than 0.325, perhaps by explaining that 0.35 is the same as 0.350? If not, how do they determine which of two decimals is greater? Are they using grids or other tools to help them decide?

- How do the players resolve disagreements about card placements? Do they try to explain their own thinking? Do they try to explain in another way if others don't understand or don't agree? Do players listen to each other's explanations and try to understand their justifications? Do players together use grids or other tools?

- What strategies do your students use to place the cards on their game mats? Do they put cards in places that optimize their opportunities for placing further cards? Do they put cards in places that make it impossible to fill other places on the board?

Fill Four

- How do your students determine how much of a grid to color to match a chosen card? Do they recognize, for example, that to represent 0.125, they color in 12½ squares on the grid? Do students use grids colored previously for assistance?

- Do students examine their partially colored grids to choose a card that will fill a grid?

- Do students correctly record below each grid the amounts they colored?

- How do students determine their scores? Do they add the totals written below each grid? Do they count the total number of unfilled squares on their four grids and compare with the number of unfilled squares of their partners?

Decimals In-Between

- What approaches do students use to order the decimals?

- Do they use fraction or percent equivalents to help them place decimals?

Capture Decimals

- How do students decide which of two cards is greater? Do students recognize that some decimals with more digits denote smaller amounts than others with fewer digits? For example, can they compare 0.4 with 0.325?

Sessions 3 and 4 Follow-Up

 **Homework**

Decimal Games   Send home several more copies of Grids, Set B of the Decimal Cards, and a copy of Decimal Grids for students to use as a reference when they play Fill Two or Fill Four with someone at home.

Fractions to Decimals

What Happens

Students find decimals of up to three digits that have a value between that of two given decimals. Students then find decimal equivalents for fractions on the calculator, making a Fraction to Decimal Division Table for all fractions with numerators and denominators from 1 to 12. They identify and explain patterns within the table. Their work focuses on:

■ finding decimals in between the value of other decimals

■ finding decimal equivalents for common fractions, including fractions greater than 1

■ recognizing fractions greater than, less than, and equal to 1

■ finding and explaining patterns in a division table

 Ten-Minute Math: Exploring Data Once or twice in the next few days and during Investigation 4, continue to do Exploring Data with your students. This time, concentrate on the Categories and Familiar Fractions variations.

For example, students choose a question and collect categorical data: perhaps a favorite sport or form of exercise, names of countries or names of states students have been in, or occupation of an adult they admire.

Encourage students to group their results into fewer, more descriptive categories, so that they can see other things about the data. For example, if the question is what states the students have been in, they might find that many states mentioned have been visited by only one or two students. If they group states by parts of the country (for example, Midwest, Southeast), they will probably find more things to say about the data.

Once data is grouped into two or three categories, students can describe the amounts as fractions, then relate them to familiar fractions and percents.

Keep the results of these surveys for use during Investigation 4.

For complete directions, see p. 126.

Materials

■ Student Sheet 21 (1 per student, and 1 transparency)

■ Calculators (1 per student)

■ Overhead projector

■ Student Sheet 22 (1 per student, homework)

Comparing Decimals

To provide practice in approximating unfamiliar decimals, ask students for examples of decimals that are not included in the deck of Decimal Cards.

The deck of Decimal Cards has examples of 39 decimal numbers, but there are many others. Give me an example of a decimal that is larger than 0.5 and smaller than 0.525.

Write 0.5 and 0.525 on the board. As students give examples, ask them to share their reasoning. Then write on the board other pairs of numbers for them to find decimals between. For example:

0.25 and 0.275   0.925 and 0.95   0 and 0.025

You might make this a collaborative effort, with each group of three or four students finding one decimal between each pair.

After students share some examples, ask three students to each give you a random digit. Write each digit on the board so a three-digit decimal is formed.

Who can read this decimal?

Students might read a three-place decimal, such as 0.736, as "point seven three six." Explain that this digit-by-digit form is a fine way to read a decimal to someone who is writing it down, but that we can also read this decimal using language that indicates its value: "seven hundred thirty-six thousandths."

Now help students make sense of the three-digit decimal on the board by relating it to more familiar "landmark" numbers:

About how large is this number? Tell me a fraction, a percent, or a decimal that is a little smaller than this number and one that is a little larger.

Students work with partners and others near them to approximate the decimal to a familiar fraction and to name one decimal that is a little larger and another one that is smaller. Circulate and observe. Are students making sensible interpretations of these decimals? For example, if the decimal were 0.736, do the students equate it with a number slightly smaller than ¾ or 75 percent? Repeat this activity several times with other three-place decimals. If the students are having difficulty, try some two-place decimals first.

Making a Division Table

Show the transparency of Student Sheet 21, Fraction to Decimal Division Table, on the overhead.

This is a division table. It is similar to a multiplication table: The numbers we start with are shown across the top and down the left side, and the answers are recorded in the inside boxes. You can use this division table for recording fraction and decimal equivalents. The numbers in the top row represent *numerators* of fractions. The numbers in the left column are *denominators*.

Model the procedure for completing the table. For example, point to 1 in the top row and 2 in the left column, ask students what fraction that would represent, what the decimal equivalent is (0.5), and where that number should be recorded. Then ask in what other boxes we can write 0.5.

Name some decimals that students found in the previous activity. For each one, ask:

What fraction does this decimal represent? So where can we write this decimal in the table?

Remind students that they found decimal equivalents in Session 1 on their calculators.

How can we find decimal equivalents for some other fractions, such as 1/7?

Distribute Student Sheet 21, Fraction to Decimal Division Table, for students to complete. Students start by filling in decimal equivalents for fractions they already know *before* using a calculator to fill in other cells of the table. Also encourage them to stop and look for patterns that will help them complete the table without a calculator.

Decimals That Fill the Display In working with calculators previously, students will have come across decimals that fill the display, and they will certainly produce some as they find decimal equivalents for fractions. For such decimals, students may write as many decimal places as will conveniently fit in the cell.

Introduce a discussion of these decimals by looking at 0.3333333.

What do you think the decimal equivalent of 1/3 means? How is it similar or different from the percent for 1/3 (331/3%)?

Students share their explanations. At this point, don't emphasize the difference between terminating and repeating decimals; see the **Teacher Note, Decimal Equivalents of Fractions (p. 90),** for a discussion of this issue. Do ask students to compare decimals that show many digits on the calculator to decimals with fewer digits.

Some people look at a decimal with many digits and think it is very big. Look at these two decimals. *[Write 0.375 and 0.3333333 on the board.]* **Which is greater? How do you know?**

Students share their thoughts and reasons why they think one decimal is greater than the other. If students disagree, suggest that they compare the fraction equivalents of these decimals (3/8 and 1/3) using their Fraction Tracks or their Percent Equivalents Strips.

You might introduce the standard recording notation for repeating decimals, a line over the repeating digit. Thus:

$$\frac{5}{12} = 0.41666666\dots \text{ is recorded as } 0.41\overline{6}$$

$$\frac{1}{3} = 0.33333333\dots \text{ is recorded as } 0.\overline{3}$$

Observing the Students The Fraction to Decimal Division Table gives you a chance to see how your students think mathematically. As you circulate, ask individuals to explain how they are figuring out the decimals. Observe the order in which students complete the table:

■ Do they start by filling in the decimals they already know from earlier activities?

■ Do they fill in whole rows using patterns, such as knowing that the row for the denominator 2 (or the halves row) increases by steps of 0.5?

■ Do they recognize and fill in the diagonal on the table, for fractions equivalent to the number 1?

Activity

Patterns in the Division Table

When students have completed the Fraction to Decimal Division Table, they work in small groups to compare their tables and check their entries *without using a calculator.* When students disagree about an entry, they discuss and justify what the entry must be—why a particular decimal is sensible for that fraction, or how the patterns in the table support that entry. Circulate to listen to students' arguments. When they use a pattern to justify an entry, ask them to also explain why that pattern makes sense.

When students have had a few minutes to compare their tables, call them together to share with the whole class some of the ways they determined entries without a calculator, and why some of the patterns they noticed occur. One way you might do this is to ask students what patterns they found useful and make a list. Then ask them to work in pairs or small groups to write why these patterns occur. Write out some of the patterns in your words, ending with "because..." for the students to complete. For example:

- The number 1 is down the diagonal because... *the number is divided by the same number and that's always 1.*

- As you read across any row, the numbers get larger because... *the top number is bigger so there are more of the decimal pieces. It's like when we did the percent lists. 20 percent is ¹/₅, and 40 percent is ²/₅.*

- As you read down any column, the numbers get smaller because... *the denominator is bigger. You make more pieces so the pieces are smaller.*

- Sixths and twelfths are the only fractions in the table with both "long" and "short" decimals because... *when you divide by a number that multiplies to 12, like 4, it stops, but numbers like 7 always make long decimals.*

Name   Date

Student Sheet 21

Fraction to Decimal Division Table

Numerator

N/D	1	2	3	4	5	6	7	8	9	10	11	12
1	1	2	3	4	5	6	7	8	9	10	11	12
2	0.5	1	1.5	2	2.5	3	3.5	4	4.5	5	5.5	6
3	0.3333	0.666	1	1.333	1.666	2	2.333	2.666	3	3.333	3.666	4
4	0.25	0.5	0.75	1	1.25	1.50	1.75	2	2.25	2.50	2.75	3
5	0.2	0.4	0.6	0.8	1	1.2	1.4	1.6	1.8	2	2.2	2.4
6	0.166	0.333	0.5	0.666	0.8333	1	1.1666	1.333	1.5	1.666	1.8333	2
7	0.1428571	0.2857142	0.4285714	0.5714285	0.7142857	0.8571428	1	1.1428571	1.2857142	1.4285714	1.5714285	1.7142857
8	0.125	0.25	0.375	0.5	0.625	0.75	0.875	1	1.125	1.25	1.375	1.5
9	0.1111	0.222	0.333	0.444	0.555	0.666	0.777	0.888	1	1.1111	1.222	1.333
10	0.1	0.2	0.3	0.4	0.5	0.6	0.7	0.8	0.9	1	1.1	1.2
11	0.0909	0.1818	0.2727	0.3636	0.4545	0.5454	0.6363	0.7272	0.8181	0.9090	1	1.0909
12	0.08333	0.16666	0.25	0.33333	0.416666	0.5	0.583333	0.66666	0.75	0.8333	0.91666	1

Denominator

© Dale Seymour Publications®

Investigation 3 • Sessions 5–6
Name That Portion

Students may discover some patterns that they can't explain but find intriguing. Interested students should be encouraged to speculate about such patterns, but don't expect them to figure out why these patterns occur. For example:

- The repeating two digits in the elevenths row are the numerator times 9; and pairs of repeating digits in the ninths row are the numerator times 11.
- The repeating digits in the sevenths row are always in the same order, but begin with a different number. That is, $1/7 = 0.142857$, $2/7 = 0.285714$, $3/7 = 0.428571$, and so on. If students spot this pattern, can they tell how they would know which digit to start with in each cell as they move across the sevenths row?

Examining Decimals Greater Than One If you have time, focus on the mixed numbers and decimals greater than 1 in the table. The **Dialogue Box,** How Much Is Nine Halves? (p. 91), shows how one teacher started this discussion. Here are some other questions you might ask students to consider:

- Can you find a decimal number in the table that is slightly greater than $3\frac{1}{2}$?
- Which is the smallest decimal in the table that is greater than 1?
- The fractions $8/7$ and $7/5$ are both between 1 and 2. Without looking at your table, which do you think is larger? Why do you think so? What is the decimal representation of $8/7$? *[Write 1.1428571 on the board.]* What is the decimal representation for $7/5$? *[Write 1.4 on the board.]* Which decimal is larger? How do you know by looking at the decimal?

Students might work together to put some mixed numbers and numbers with repeating digits in order, from smallest to largest, without looking at their tables. For example:

1.1111111	0.2222222	3.6666666
0.3636363	1.375	1.1666666

Afterward, students share their strategies.

Sessions 5 and 6 Follow-Up

Fraction, Decimal, Percent Equivalents   Students take home Student Sheet 22, Fraction, Decimal, Percent Equivalents, and complete the chart.

🏠 **Homework**

🗗 **Extensions**

Guess My Fraction   For this game, two pairs of students play together as teams. Each team chooses a fraction with both the numerator and the denominator less than or equal to 10 and uses the calculator to find the decimal equivalent. They write the decimal result of their division on paper and trade with the other team. The challenge for each team is to find a fraction that gives the decimal result of the other team's division. After both teams have found an answer, they discuss and record the strategies they used. In searching for a fraction to match 0.625, for example, they might give a strategy like one of these:

> It is littler than 1 so we knew the top number (numerator) had to be smaller than the bottom number (denominator).

> It was bigger than 0.5 so we knew the numerator had to be more than ½ the denominator.

Some students may be surprised when the fraction they find is not the original; for 0.25, they may find ¼ when the other team started with ²⁄₈. They should be able to satisfy each other that the two are equivalent.

Fraction Calculators   If you have fraction calculators, such as the Math Explorer, allow time for student exploration of how they work. Below are the keys they will find particularly useful.

| / | Separates the numerator from the denominator: $2/3$ |

| Unit | Enters the whole-number portion of a mixed number: $1u\,3/4$ |

| F◌D | Changes a fraction to a decimal, and vice versa:
2.25 | F◌D | becomes $2u25/100$ |

| Ab/c | Converts a fraction to a mixed number:
$11/4$ | Ab/c | becomes $2u3/4$ |

| Simp | = | Simplifies fractions; expresses fraction in lower terms:
$25/100$ | Simp | = | becomes $5/20$ |

Students can try finding fraction-decimal equivalencies with the fraction calculator. They might also try some of the addition and subtraction problems they wrote in earlier investigations.

Since all fractions are one way to represent the division of two numbers, using calculators makes finding decimal equivalents of fractions very easy. However, it is important that your students develop some understanding of what the results indicate. When the denominator of a fraction is a factor of the numerator, as in $^{25}/_5$, the decimal equivalent is a whole number. In all other cases, there will be at least one number following the decimal point.

As your students use calculators to find decimal equivalents of fractions, they will notice that decimal equivalents for these fractions fall into two main groups—decimals that terminate, or end after a certain number of digits, and decimals that fill the calculator display and seem to go on beyond the digits on the display.

All nonterminating decimal equivalents of fractions are called repeating decimals—some or all of the decimal digits repeat. For $^5/_6$ or $0.8\overline{3}$ (0.833333...), only the 3 repeats. For $^2/_{11}$ or $0.\overline{18}$ (0.181818...), two digits repeat. For some fractions, such as $^1/_3$ ($0.\overline{3}$) or $^1/_6$ ($.1\overline{6}$), the repeating pattern is quite obvious; for others, such as $^1/_7$ ($0.\overline{142857}$), it is not. Identifying the repeating pattern is not necessarily easy. For example, $^{47}/_{49}$ begins 0.9591 and goes on for 42 decimal places before it repeats all 42 digits. There is no way of knowing this from an eight-digit calculator display.

For some nonterminating decimals, there is no repeating pattern; these are irrational numbers (numbers that cannot be expressed as the division of two whole numbers). Pi (π) and the square root of 2 are examples of irrational numbers.

In this unit, avoid emphasizing that all fractions will be either terminating or repeating decimals. At this age, your students will have no way of proving why this is true, and there is a danger they will decide that things that appear to be true for a certain number of cases can be generalized as a "proof" for all cases. For example, for repeating decimals, students may assume—incorrectly—that the reappearance of a single digit in a decimal indicates the start of a repeating pattern. This is true for single-digit denominators; for $^1/_7$, most calculators display 0.1428571, and the second 1 is the beginning of the repeating pattern. But the rule doesn't always work for denominators with more than one digit; $^{47}/_{49}$ obviously has many digits occurring more than once in the 42 digits of its repeating pattern.

How Much Is Nine Halves?

While filling in Student Sheet 21, Fraction to Decimal Division Table (p. 163), this class has been using mental math and pencil and paper, along with their calculators, to find the decimal equivalents of many fractions. The teacher wants the students to think about "top heavy" fractions—those with numerators that are larger than the denominators.

Some of the fractions in this table are less than 1 whole, and some are more. *[The teacher writes 10/4 on the board.]* **Is this more or less than 1?** *[There's disagreement.]* **A lot of you think it is less than 1. Becky, what makes you think it is more than 1?**

Becky: Because 10 is greater than 4. Four goes into it more than one time, so it's more than 1 whole.

Try another one. [*The teacher writes 9/2.*] **Bigger or less than 1? Think about it: 9 divided by 2. How else could you show it, besides like this** *[points to the fractional form]*? **If I said show me, or show a third grader, how would you break it up?**

Mei-Ling: Two halves is a whole. *[The teacher records 1/2 + 1/2 = 1.]* And then go on and on, 9 times. [*The teacher writes 1/2 + 1/2 + 1/2 + 1/2 + 1/2 + 1/2 + 1/2 + 1/2 + 1/2.*]

Katrina: Now put the halves together. I put two halves together, and that gives me a whole. *[The teacher circles 1/2 + 1/2 and puts 1 under it; then does this three more times.]* Four wholes and a half more. That's 4 1/2.

So what answer do you think you would get on your calculators?

Christine: Four point five (4.5).

Now try 9/8.

Zach: If you had cakes, and you split the cakes up, there's one cake in 8 pieces and 1 piece more.

Mei-Ling: One-eighth is 12 1/2 percent. So if we write 12 1/2 nine times... *[The teacher writes 12 1/2 + 12 1/2 + 12 1/2 + 12 1/2 + 12 1/2 + 12 1/2 + 12 1/2 + 12 1/2 + 12 1/2 and Mei-Ling starts adding them together, in pairs, as percents]* 25, 50, 75, 100... *[The teacher writes 25 under each pair.]* So 9/8 is more than 1 because it's over 100.

Mei-Ling took 2 eighths and saw them as 1 quarter. How would you put that on your paper? How could you break down 9 eighths for a younger child?

Heather: Add the 12 1/2's. Add all the halves first. So... 4 wholes and a half. *[The teacher writes 4 1/2.]* And then add the wholes, the 12's... *[she calculates on her paper]* 108. *[The teacher writes 108 near the 4 1/2.]* So 112 1/2.

How can I show that this *[points to 112 1/2]* **is the same as 1 1/8? Can you change that into 9/8?**

Amir: One hundred percent is a whole. That leaves 12 1/2 percent left, and that's 1/8, like we started with.

Fraction, Percent, and Decimal Problems

Materials

- Student Sheet 23 (1 per student)
- Students' previous fraction work (for reference)
- Student Sheet 24 (1 per student, homework)
- Calculators (available)

What Happens

Students solve word problems involving fractions, decimals, and percents, and share their strategies. They also discuss any changes in the ranking of the sports teams they have been following. Their work focuses on:

- finding percents and fractional parts of whole numbers
- computing with fractions, decimals, and percents
- making sense of and solving word problems
- writing ratios as percents or fractions to compare them
- writing a remainder to fit the context

Activity

Scoring Sports and Other Problems

Students work individually to solve the problems on Student Sheet 23, Scoring Sports and Other Problems. They may use whatever materials and illustrations are useful to them, including calculators. Again, be sure students have their folders available, but avoid encouraging the use of any particular models.

❖ **Tip for the Linguistically Diverse Classroom** If some students need the problems read aloud, pair them with English-proficient students. As necessary, they can add sketches to the sheet to help with unfamiliar vocabulary.

Note: Students can solve the first two problems without knowing anything about the scoring of gymnastics meets. If some are unfamiliar with the terms *vault* and *floor,* you might ask others in the class to share what they know about these events. They might also be interested in knowing that the highest possible score for any event is 10. Points are always given in tenths, but when two judges' scores are averaged, a participant may receive a score in hundredths. Thus, for Jameel in problem 2, one judge might have awarded 7.6 points on the vault and the other 7.9, giving him a score of 7.75.

Observing the Students   Circulate while students are working and observe how they are thinking about and solving the problems. If students are using conventional algorithms, ask them to explain why these procedures make sense to use in this situation. The answers, along with some issues to consider and approaches to look for, are as follows:

- **Problem 1 answer:** 7.9

  Consider: Provide help with the gymnastics terms as necessary. To solve the problem, some students may write down the numbers and add; others may add them mentally. Some students may subtract the sum from 32; others may count on, or mentally add on to the sum to get to 32. If it's not apparent what students are doing, ask them to explain their thinking to you.

- **Problem 2 answer:** 1.05 better

  Consider: How do students compare two decimals with a different number of places? Do they recognize that the difference is 1.05, and do they know how to write it?

- **Problem 3 answer:** 6 runners

  Consider: How do students solve this problem that is typically considered to be a division problem? If students are having difficulty, encourage them to make a drawing or describe and act out the situation.

- **Problem 4 answers: (a)** $3.25 **(b)** $3\frac{1}{4}$ feet, or 3 feet 3 inches **(c)** 4 cars

  Consider: Can students express remainders to match the context of the situation? If students only record numerical answers, read the questions to them and ask them to interpret their answer as it relates to each situation.

- **Problem 5 answer:** Eva is slightly better, because her 4 out of 12 hits is $\frac{1}{3}$ or $33\frac{1}{3}\%$, and Ryan's 3 out of 10 hits is $\frac{3}{10}$ or 30%.

  Consider: Do students express each person's hits as fractions? How do they compare the two fractions to know which is larger (better)? Do they use any tools or models from the unit?

- **Problem 6 answer:** Less than the national data, because $\frac{10}{30} = 33\frac{1}{3}\%$, which is less than 39%.

  Consider: Do students know how to use data given in the problem to make a percent? The most likely error will be for students to express the "10 have dogs" as 10 percent.

When students have finished, discuss their strategies for finding solutions. Because decimals are the particular topic of this investigation, you might focus on alternative strategies for adding and subtracting decimals, as in problems 1 and 2.

Team Rankings

Take a few minutes to review the data students have been collecting for activity begun in Session 1, Win/Loss Records. If you have not been collecting data on a class chart, write on the board the most recent data students have brought in. What percentages have they found for their teams? Have the numbers been changing? Have the team rankings changed? Which team has the best record? the worst?

Session 7 Follow-Up

Homework

Comparing Common Fractions   Explain that in the next session, the class will be making posters that show many ways to compare two fractions, such as 2/3 and 2/5. For homework, students start planning this. Ask them to think of ways to convince someone that 2/3 is larger than 2/5. Students write their ideas on Student Sheet 24, Comparing Common Fractions, and bring them in to share at the beginning of Session 8.

Extension

Fraction, Percent, and Decimal Equivalents   Students challenge themselves and their classmates to find fraction, percent, and decimal equivalents. They make charts with one or two values provided in each row and work together or on their own to fill in the missing entries. For example:

Fraction	Percent	Decimal
$\frac{2}{5}$		
	175%	
	$33\frac{1}{3}\%$	$0.\overline{3}$

Comparing Fractional Amounts

Materials

- Large sheets of paper
- Colored pencils, crayons, or markers (assortment to share)
- A supply of Grids, Clock Fractions, Decimal Grids, fraction strips in five colors
- Students' Percent Equivalents Strips and completed Grids sheets (for reference)
- Student Sheet 25 (1 per student, homework)
- Calculators (available)

What Happens

In an assessment activity that draws on students' experiences in the first three investigations, small groups make posters that show many ways to compare two fractional amounts. They may use any notations or models they find useful to support their arguments. Their work focuses on:

- representing fractions in different ways
- comparing common fractions and mixed numbers
- using equivalent fractions, percents, and decimals

Activity

Assessment

Showing Which Is Larger

In this session, students make posters to convince people that something they know about fractions, percents, and decimals is true. Talk about the ideas they generated for homework at the end of Session 7, and use these to model the writing of convincing statements to support their comparisons of fractions.

Let's say you have a friend or relative who is still puzzled by fractions, percents, and decimals. How could you convince this person that ⅔ is larger than ⅖?

On chart paper or the board, list the explanations students found for homework.

....

❖ **Tip for the Linguistically Diverse Classroom** To make each explanation comprehensible, add visual aids, either by taping actual examples to the chart or by sketching fraction strips, rectangles cut into thirds and sixths, shaded circles and clock faces, and so on.

....

Title this list *Why Two-Thirds Is Larger Than Two-Fifths,* or

Why $\frac{2}{3} > \frac{2}{5}$

This is a chance to use the greater than (>) and less than (<) signs and to encourage students to use them. If students have trouble remembering which is which, point out that the wide-open side faces the larger number and the little point faces the smaller number (5 < 10, 10 > 5).

WHY $\frac{2}{3} > \frac{2}{5}$

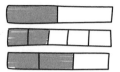

- $\frac{1}{2}$ is bigger than $\frac{2}{5}$, and $\frac{2}{3}$ is bigger than $\frac{1}{2}$. We can see that on the fraction strips.

- $\frac{2}{5}$ is 40%, and $\frac{2}{3}$ is $66\frac{2}{3}$%.

- Make two circles. Mark one in thirds and one in fifths. Fill in two pieces on both.

- Thirds are larger than fifths because when you cut something into more pieces, each piece is smaller.

- $\frac{2}{3}$ of an hour is 40 minutes. $\frac{2}{5}$ of an hour is two 12 minutes, which is 24 minutes.

- As decimals, $\frac{2}{3}$ is 0.666666 and $\frac{2}{5}$ is just 0.4 (or 0.400000).

Divide the class into groups of three to six students to work on their posters. Each poster should present at least as many justifications of which fraction is larger as there are students in the group. Following are some fraction pairs they could focus on; you might suggest a different fraction pair to each group.

Easier pairs	More difficult pairs
$\frac{2}{5}$ and $\frac{2}{3}$	$\frac{5}{6}$ and $\frac{7}{8}$
$\frac{1}{2}$ and $\frac{2}{5}$	$\frac{3}{4}$ and $\frac{7}{10}$
$\frac{3}{4}$ and $\frac{4}{3}$	$\frac{12}{5}$ and $\frac{7}{3}$
$\frac{3}{4}$ and $\frac{7}{8}$	$\frac{1}{3}$ and $\frac{2}{5}$
$\frac{5}{2}$ and $\frac{10}{3}$	$\frac{5}{8}$ and $\frac{3}{5}$

As students begin planning their posters, encourage them to think about how to use percents and decimals and how to make use of some of the visual models they have used. Make available copies of grids and clocks they can cut out and use on their posters. Encourage them to draw pictures as well. Suggest that they refer to work in their math folders for ideas. Students may use a calculator in one of their justifications, but they must show the computation problem they did and interpret the answer they got.

Once they are working, circulate and ask students about the different statements they are using. Insist that they be clear so you are convinced by each justification of which fraction is larger.

Some groups may have time to compare more than one pair, or you might assign an addition or subtraction problem for students to explain in many ways (see the Extension, Showing Fraction Addition and Subtraction, p. 99).

Evaluating the Posters Observing students while they work and reviewing their posters will help you assess students' understanding of fractions and their decimal and percent equivalents. Consider:

- What fractions did students choose to compare? (And, if they did the extension, what computation problems did they choose to solve?) Did they choose items that are relatively simple, or items that are more challenging to explain?

- How clear are students' explanations? Do the explanations provide evidence that students understand fractions?

- Did the students use decimal or percent equivalents of fractions in meaningful ways?

- What models or ways did students use to explain their thinking? For example, did they relate their comparison or problem to real-life situations? Did they use grids, clocks, fractions strips, fraction tracks, calculators, or other tools to support their explanations?

- Were students able to use a number of different models or ways to explain their thinking? Do all their ways make sense?

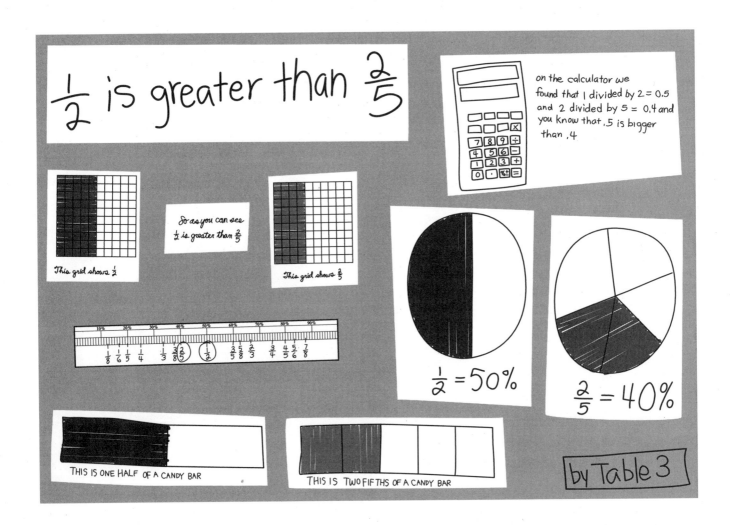

If there is time, bring the class together for each group to show and explain their poster. Since these posters are designed to communicate with others, you might post them in the hall.

Save extra pages and partial pages of grids, clocks, and strips for students to use for homework.

Session 8 Follow-Up

More Fraction Comparisons Students decide, with your advice, on one or two fraction pairs to compare at home. They write the two fractions and write or draw two or more convincing statements for how they know which fraction is larger on Student Sheet 25, More Fraction Comparisons.

 **Homework**

Showing Fraction Addition and Subtraction Students make posters similar to those comparing two fractions, but this time demonstrating different ways to explain and find the answer to one of the following addition and subtraction problems.

 **Extension**

Easier problems: $\frac{1}{6} + \frac{1}{3}$ $\frac{2}{3} + \frac{1}{6}$ $\frac{3}{4} - \frac{1}{2}$ $3 + 1\frac{1}{4}$

More difficult problems: $\frac{1}{5} + \frac{1}{4}$ $\frac{3}{8} + \frac{3}{4}$ $\frac{5}{6} - \frac{1}{3}$ $3 - 1\frac{1}{4}$

INVESTIGATION 4 (EXCURSION)

Data and Percents in Circle Graphs

A Note on Investigation 4

This investigation offers a final project for this unit. You may either do the project as a culmination of the unit or choose to do it later in the year, as your schedule permits.

What Happens

Session 1: Planning Age or Gender Surveys

Students use a variety of methods to find the percentage breakdown of their class by groups (adults/children and males/females). They brainstorm places or activities where they think the participation rates of two groups might be about equal and where they might be quite different. Students then plan a survey, to be conducted outside of class, to investigate hypotheses they have made about these groups.

Session 2: Circle Graphs
Students make circle graphs to represent two groups of data. They use a marked transparent circle (a "Percentractor") to identify the size of the sectors for each graph.

Sessions 3 and 4: Interpreting Percents
In Choice Time, students work on three activities: they match given data to unlabeled circle graphs; they decide whether certain statements about percents are possible or impossible; and they begin preparing reports on their survey results.

Sessions 5 and 6: Survey Reports
Students finish preparing their survey reports, showing the results for each of three questions as familiar fractions, as percents, and in circle graphs. Groups share their reports with the class by posting them for others to review and by orally sharing a few of their conclusions.

Session 7: Two Days in My Life
Students describe a typical day in their life today (as children) and as they imagine their life will be at age 30 (as adults). They classify their daily activities into categories and determine the number of hours and the fraction and percent of the day for each category. They make circle graphs to show the results.

Mathematical Emphasis

- planning and conducting surveys
- organizing and representing data as fractions, percents, and in circle graphs
- interpreting common uses of fractions, decimals, and percents

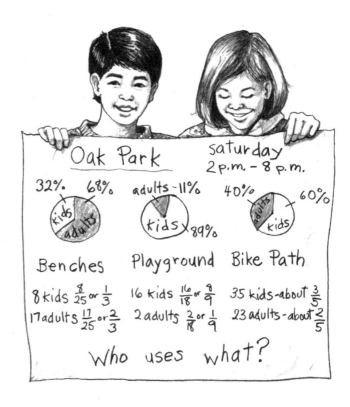

What to Plan Ahead of Time

Materials

- Scissors: 1 per student (Sessions 2, 5–6)
- Overhead projector (Session 2)
- Large paper (about 11 by 17 inches) for making reports: 1 per group (Sessions 5–6)
- Crayons or markers (Sessions 5–6)
- Glue (Sessions 5–6)
- Large stick-on notes: several per student (Sessions 5–6)

Other Preparation

- Read the **Teacher Note,** Planning the Surveys (p. 109), before starting this investigation.
- Duplicate student sheets and teaching resources (located at the end of this unit) in the following quantities. If you have Student Activity Booklets, copy only the items marked with an asterisk.

For Session 1

Student Sheet 26, Survey Plans (p. 171): 1 per student

For Session 2

Circle Graphs (p. 176): 2 per student and 1 transparency*

Percentractors* (p. 177): 1 transparency per 6 students

For Sessions 3–4

Student Sheet 27, Matching Data to Circle Graphs (p. 172): 1 per student

Student Sheet 28, Possible or Impossible? (p. 173): 1 per student

For Sessions 5–6

Circle Graphs* (p. 176): 1 sheet per group, optional

For Session 7

Student Sheet 29, Typical Daily Schedules (p. 174): 1 per student

Student Sheet 30, Two Typical Days in My Life (p. 175): 1 per student

- For Session 2, prepare a transparent Percentractor (p. 177) for demonstration

Planning Age or Gender Surveys

Materials

- Student Sheet 26 (1 per student)

What Happens

Students use a variety of methods to find the percentage breakdown of their class by groups (adults/children and males/females). They brainstorm places or activities where they think the participation rates of two groups might be about equal and where they might be quite different. Students then plan a survey, to be conducted outside of class, to investigate hypotheses they have made about these groups. Their work focuses on:

- representing a population as fractions and percents
- choosing survey questions
- planning how to collect data

Age and Gender Distributions

In this investigation, students design surveys to collect comparative data about two groups: either males and females, or adults and children. Characterizing groups of people by the things they do is similar to the marketing research that advertisers use. Hold a brief discussion of this before introducing the students' surveys.

People who sell things have to decide when and where to advertise their product. Often they use *market research* to help them make these decisions. Market research involves taking surveys. The surveys might collect data on the things people do, the things they read, the things they eat, what they watch on TV. These data are usually expressed as percents. For example, suppose someone took a survey on the TV programs that fifth grade boys and girls watch.

As you describe some hypothetical survey results for three TV programs, write them on the board.

Program A	Program B	Program C
36% girls	62% girls	48% girls
64% boys	38% boys	52% boys

If you wanted to advertise a new bike helmet especially for girls, which would be the best program to advertise on? Why? How were these numbers in percents useful to you?

Ask if anyone can suggest another situation in which taking a survey could help a company that wanted to sell or advertise something. As necessary, suggest some other ideas yourself.

Suppose you made new cars, and could make them in only four colors. How would you decide what colors to offer? How could a market research survey help you choose the four colors that would sell best? Would it help you to know what percent of the people who buy your car are males and what percent are females? (It might help, especially if you knew from another survey that color preferences vary by gender.)

Suppose you made a new brand of microwave pizza. What might you learn from a survey that would help you market this pizza? Think in terms of percents. (For example, what percent of people own microwave ovens; what percent of people like pizza; what percents like various toppings, and so forth.)

Data Expressed as Percents   Survey results are nearly always reported as percents. In order to analyze and compare the results from their surveys, students will be turning their raw data into percents. Briefly review this process.

Suppose we were collecting data about the people in our classroom. How many people do we have in the room altogether? What fraction of the people are adults? What fraction are children? What fraction are males? What fraction are females?

Record student responses on the board, first as fractions. For example, in a class with 28 students and 1 teacher, 1/29 of the people are adults and 28/29 are children. If the teacher is a man and 15 students are boys, then 16/29 of the people are males and 13/29 are females. Ask students to relate numbers like these to more familiar fractions.

What do these fractions mean? Are they close to any fractions that are more familiar, like 1/2 or 2/3 or 3/4?

How could we express these fractions as percents?

Students work in pairs or small groups to determine the percents that describe the distribution of people in their classroom: the percent who are adults and the percent who are children, and the percents who are males and females.

As students suggest particular percents, they explain their strategies. Some students will simply approximate, saying, for example, that the class is 99% children and 1% adults. In a class with 15/32 girls and 17/32 boys, some students said the percents seemed to be about 40% female and 60% male. Other students in the same class focused on familiar fractions for the number of boys and girls in the class, and because both fractions were very close to ½, thought that the percent for each would be closer to 50%.

Another class related the specific fractions to familiar fractions and then used their Percent Equivalents Strips to find the percents. Others found percents by dividing on a calculator (say, the number of adults or the number of children divided by the number of people in the class) and expressing the decimal answer as an equivalent percent.

Whatever strategy they used, some students found percents separately for the two groups; others found one of the percents, then subtracted from 100 to find the other percent.

$$\frac{18}{30} = 60\% \text{ female} \qquad 100\% - 60\% = 40\% \text{ male}$$

Activity

Making Age or Gender Hypotheses

Students begin the survey project by brainstorming lists of things people do. As they think of activities, they should also be thinking about the participants: Are they mostly males, mostly females, or are there about equal numbers of both? Is this something done mostly by adults, mostly by children, or by equal numbers of both? You might want the whole class to focus on the same groupings (either age or gender), or you could introduce both and let working groups choose their own focus for their survey.

Think of some places where people go—maybe to buy things, or just for fun. And think of different things people do, such as driving a car, cooking, playing soccer, watching sports, reading books, taking photographs, and so forth.

Also think about people you see on TV or in magazines—maybe people in commercials, or in different types of shows.

For some places or activities, the number of males and females (or adults and children) you would see is probably about equal. For other places or activities, you might expect to see many more of one group or the other.

Make some hypotheses. Where do you think the groups will be about equal? Where will one group be more heavily represented than the other? Tell me your ideas, and I'll record them on the board.

As needed, give examples of related hypotheses, such as these:

> There are about an equal number of adults and children in TV ads during prime-time comedy shows.
>
> There are more children in TV ads during cartoon shows.
>
> There are more adults in TV ads during news programs.

> There will be more males than females in a sports card shop.
>
> There will be more females than males in a shoe store.
>
> There will be about the same number of males and females in a book store.

Students' ideas might center on age or gender differences in the people who frequent different kinds of stores or who attend different types of special events (ball games, concerts, plays); age or gender differences among people who ride bikes or use in-line skates, or who collect different types of things; age or gender differences among people who read certain kinds of books or magazines, or who see certain kinds of movies; age or gender differences in who does different types of tasks around the home, and so forth.

Because students will be making three hypotheses for their surveys, encourage them to think of parallel items that are part of larger categories. For example, if they suggest an activity at the park, ask if they can think of three things at the park—one that might attract more children than grownups (the playground), one that might attract more grownups (the park benches), and one with equal numbers of both groups (the picnic tables).

As students suggest their hypotheses, others in the class may disagree. Point out that these ideas are only *hypotheses*—what people think might be the case—and that students will soon have an opportunity to test some of their hypotheses.

During this part of the project, especially when discussing gender differences, encourage students to be nonjudgmental. It should be clear that one activity is not better than another because one gender has a higher participation rate, and that higher numbers of one gender for an activity does not mean the other gender is or should be excluded. See the **Teacher Note**, Dealing with Gender Issues (p. 108), for more on gender stereotypes, which are often magnified by market research and advertising.

Making Survey Plans

For this survey project, students will be working in small groups of three or four. You may prefer to have students work in groups that are already established in your class, you may want to let students choose new groups, or you may establish groups based on students' survey interests. Distribute Student Sheet 26, Survey Plans, to each group, and read through it together.

You and your group are going to investigate some hypotheses about the types of people who participate in a certain activity, or who are represented in different ways on TV or in magazines.

Each group needs to choose one place or activity where they predict one group will predominate, one where they think the other group will predominate, and one where they expect about an equal number of each group.

It's best if the three things you choose to investigate are related to one another. For example, your group may choose to survey different kinds of stores in a mall, or different activities on the playground, or people pictured in different types of advertisements on TV or in magazines.

After you have decided what to survey, write down hypotheses for your three predictions. For each hypothesis, you need to guess the percent you will find for each group.

Your students may need some guidance as they write their hypotheses and determine how they will collect data. This project can be quite ambitious, or it can be handled very simply. Some topics will require on-site observations. Other hypotheses may require students to review printed material or television programs. See the **Teacher Note**, Planning the Surveys (p. 109), for some tips.

You will need to plan how you will conduct your investigation. For example, what could you do to find out:

- **the number of male and female customers in a store in a mall?**
- **the percent of children and adults who play video games in the arcade?**
- **the percent of female and male reporters on TV news programs?**

After students collect their data, they will be preparing reports on their findings. Student Sheet 26 provides a checklist of things to be included in the reports. As they plan their surveys, they will want to consider the requirements for the final report.

Allow time for groups to discuss and decide what they want to investigate and to plan how they will conduct their survey. If students work in groups of four, you might suggest forming two pairs to conduct their surveys at different times or locations. For example, if a group decides to survey grocery stores, the two pairs may count the number of male and female shoppers at different stores, or they may decide to observe shoppers in the same store at different times or on different days. They write their plans on the back of Student Sheet 26.

Observing the Students Walk around and listen as students plan their surveys. Discuss with them the details of how they will conduct their surveys and whether their results will allow them to answer one of these two questions:

What percent are males and what percent are females?

What percent are children and what percent are adults?

Students who are focusing on age differences may need to spend some time defining the two groups, *children* and *adults*. Where will they draw the line? Are teenagers children or adults? For borderline cases, how can they decide without asking a person's age?

If a group's question is not related to a particular site or media situation, ask them who they plan to survey—all the students in the school? all the students in their class? all the fifth graders in the school? Ask them to consider whether they think the group they plan to survey is representative of the school, or whether their school is representative of young people in the United States. It is important that students do not choose particular individuals as survey subjects. To limit the scope of their task, they might choose a certain duration of time (say, 1 hour) or a certain number of people (say, the first 20 or 50) for their survey, but to keep the survey impartial, they may not make a list of people to survey.

Students need to be sure to record the date, time, and the duration of their observations. Tell the class how many days they have to collect their data (surveys need to be completed by Session 5).

During the next three sessions, plan to check with each group daily and discuss their progress.

Session 1 Follow-Up

Surveys Students work outside of class to finish planning their surveys with others in their group. As necessary, they make arrangements with their families if they plan to conduct their survey away from school and their homes. Then they begin their surveys.

 **Homework**

During Investigation 4, students collect and compare data with two variables, focusing on differences associated either with gender (males/females) or with age (children/adults). The students' surveys are in some ways similar to market research surveys that seek to characterize people along certain lines—gender, age, income, family size, occupation, geographic region, and a host of other variables—in order to paint a picture of a "typical" consumer for a product. While such a picture may be useful to advertisers, there is a drawback to generalizing about people in this way: It quickly leads to stereotyping.

In this survey project, when students make hypotheses about the percentage of males and females they expect to find doing different things, they tend to categorize according to traditional gender roles, or stereotypes. This may raise some questions, comments, and objections from others in the class. You may want to briefly discuss stereotyping and its effects, both on those who do and on those who do not fit the pattern.

As groups plan their surveys and discuss their results, help them recognize possible stereotyping. Are there any surprises? Sometimes the percentages may show that their preconceptions were wrong. In other cases, the percentages may seem to bear out a common stereotype. Such percentages can help explain why male and female stereotypes are perpetuated by the advertising we see daily.

You can help students think further about male and female roles and activities by asking questions like these:

- If one gender does this more than the other gender, why do you think this is so? Is it because most (males/females) are uninterested in this? Are they made to feel unwelcome or uncomfortable doing this? Are both genders equally capable of doing this?

- Do (males/females) have any advantage in life because they do this? Do people of the other gender have any disadvantage because they tend not to do this?

- Is this a stereotype that we should try to change? If so, how might change come about?

Planning the Surveys

Clarifying the Questions   In this investigation, students collect data to test their hypotheses about the characteristics of two groups—either males and females, or children and adults. For many hypotheses, we can collect and graph data in at least two ways, depending on the questions we ask. One way uses a single circle graph that shows the two groups surveyed as subsets of the population as a whole. The other way uses two circle graphs, representing the two groups as separate sets. For simplicity and for ease of comparing findings, students should work toward one circle graph for each hypothesis.

As students interpret their hypotheses and gather and analyze data, they will need guidance to ensure that their results give the intended single graph. The following hypothetical example demonstrates how the same hypothesis can be interpreted in two ways.

Hypothesis: In the fourth and fifth grades in this school, about the same percent of girls and boys have read *Charlotte's Web.*

Data: The population of all fourth and fifth grade classes is 200 students (100 boys and 100 girls). All were surveyed, and 150 of the students (67 boys and 83 girls) have read *Charlotte's Web.*

Interpretation 1 (as intended in this investigation): Of the fourth and fifth grade students in this school who have read *Charlotte's Web,* what percent are girls? What percent are boys?

The resulting graph and summary sentences would look like this:

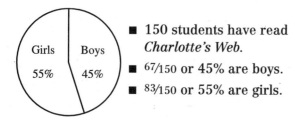

- 150 students have read *Charlotte's Web.*
- ⁶⁷/₁₅₀ or 45% are boys.
- ⁸³/₁₅₀ or 55% are girls.

Interpretation 2 (*not* intended for this investigation): Of the fourth and fifth grade girls in this school, what percent have read *Charlotte's Web?* What percent of the boys have read it?

Looking at these questions would result in two graphs and summary sentences similar to these:

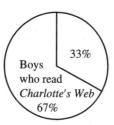

- 67 out of 100 boys, or 67%, have read *Charlotte's Web.*
- 33% of the boys have not read it.

- 83 out of 100 girls, or 83%, have read *Charlotte's Web.*
- 17% of the girls have not read it.

The goal for students is to focus on one group—people who participate in a particular activity—divided into two subgroups—the number/percent of each group who participate. Thus, the people who participate in a particular activity must be defined as the population for the survey (in this case, those who read *Charlotte's Web*); then the population must be divided into two groups (in this case, males and females).

So, for example, the data collectors might go into a fourth grade class and ask everyone who has read *Charlotte's Web* to stand up. Then they tally the number of boys and girls in that group. Those who have not read the book are not counted at all; they are not part of the population being surveyed.

Continued on next page

Monitor the groups and, if necessary, help students restate their questions to give them data that can be graphed on one circle graph representing 100 percent of the population. If your students collect data for their survey by observing only the population that participates in the activity, such as actually observing the shoppers in a book store, this issue will not arise and should not be introduced.

Conducting the Surveys   You need to decide where it is feasible for your students to conduct their surveys. In some places, it will be possible for students to go around their neighborhood or to playgrounds, stores, or malls. In other places, students will need to collect data at school or by surveying media in their homes, for example, counting the number of male and female newscasters (anchors and reporters) on all TV channels, or the number of children and adults in advertisements during Saturday morning cartoons.

If your students are going to conduct their surveys away from school and their homes, there are several considerations. First, students need to inform their parents or guardians about where they will go and what they will be doing, and obtain permission to do so. If they plan to go to a store, they need to talk to the store manager about what they want to do and obtain approval to collect data. Discuss with students how they can be unobtrusive to patrons and employees of the store. You will also want to address when and for how long a period students should collect their data.

If students are going to collect data at school, they should first identify the activity they plan to investigate, and then find a way to count only those males and females who participate. For example, they might count the students who ride bicycles to school by monitoring the bike racks; or, over several recesses, they might keep track of the students who play jump rope.

If students go into other classes to conduct their surveys, one easy and quick way to collect data is to ask all the students who participate in the target activity to stand, and then count the number of boys and girls. In this situation, students should plan carefully the form of the question they will ask. For example, the question "Do you play baseball?" may result in all students standing, whereas more specific question, such as "Are you a member of a baseball or softball team?" may produce quite different results.

Circle Graphs

What Happens

Students make circle graphs to represent two groups of data. They use a marked transparent circle (a "Percentractor") to identify the size of the sectors for each graph. Their work focuses on:

- interpreting circle graphs
- constructing circle graphs with two variables
- interpreting everyday situations that involve fractions, decimals, and percents

Materials

- Circle Graphs (2 sheets per student)
- Circle Graphs transparency
- Percentractors (1 transparency per 6 students)
- Scissors (1 per student)
- Overhead projector
- Students' Survey Plans from Session 1

For the next three sessions, students will be working with circle graphs and making sense of data expressed in percents. At the same time, they will continue to gather survey data and work on their reports.

Introduce circle graphs by showing the Circle Graphs transparency on the overhead.

One way we can show data is on circle graphs, sometimes called pie charts. For example, if our class had exactly 50 percent boys and 50 percent girls, we could show it this way. *[On the transparency, draw a line dividing one circle in half through the drawn radius, and label the two halves Boys and Girls.]*

If our class had 25 percent boys and 75 percent girls, how could we show it on a circle graph?

Ask a volunteer to show this on a circle graph on the transparency, labeling the two sections as you did. Many will see the similarity to the Fraction Clocks (introduced in Investigation 2). The similarity holds true for halves and quarters, but you will need to point out that *this* circle is divided into 10, not 12, equal parts, as tenths are useful for finding percents.

Distribute a copy of the Circle Graphs sheet to each student. Direct attention to the markings on each circle.

You can use the circles on this sheet to make circle graphs. How will the marks around the edge help you represent percents?

Activity

Making Circle Graphs

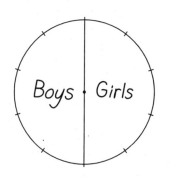

On the Circle Graphs sheet, a radius is drawn to indicate a starting point for students when making a circle graph. You might explain that the location of this starting line is arbitrary.

How would you show on a circle graph that a group is 10 percent girls and 90 percent boys?

After students explain and show how they would mark the circle graph, list the following data on the board:

> 60% bus to school, 40% walk to school
>
> 25% adults, 75% children
>
> 85% own a calculator, 15% don't own a calculator
>
> $66\frac{2}{3}$% married, $33\frac{1}{3}$% unmarried

Working in small groups, students represent these data on four circle graphs, then share their strategies for making the graphs, particularly for the last example. Did they make a mark two-thirds of the way between two lines (between 60 and 70) for the 66⅔ percent?

Introducing the "Percentractor" Show a cut-out transparent Percentractor (from p. 177) on the overhead. (*Percentractor* is a coined name, derived from combining *percent* and *protractor*. It is pronounced with the emphasis on the second syllable: per-CENT-rac-tor.)

This is a tool you can use when you make circle graphs on the Circle Graphs sheet or on paper that doesn't have circles already drawn. What do you think the solid lines and the dotted lines show?

On the overhead, place the Percentractor on top of a blank circle graph, aligning the center dots and one radius, and model its use.

If I want to show 45 percent, I place the Percentractor on top of a blank circle graph, making sure the center of the Percentractor is directly over the center of the circle. I'll start at the top, where the starting line is on the blank circle graph, and then count around, 10, 20, 30, 40, 45 percent, and put a little mark here at the edge. Now I'll remove the Percentractor and draw a line from the center of the circle graph, through the mark I've made, to the edge of the circle.

Note: The diameter of the Percentractor is smaller than the diameter of the circle graphs provided; this permits students to mark percents easily, even if a circle is cut out.

Using Circle Graphs to Represent Data

Distribute another sheet of Circle Graphs, copies of the transparent Percentractors, and scissors. Students cut apart each Percentractor sheet, and each individual cuts out a Percentractor to use.

List three or four sets of data you have collected during the Ten-Minute Math, Exploring Data activities (or quickly collect some data now) for students to represent on circle graphs. Use data with only two or three categories, such as students who ride the bus to school and those who do not; students who were born in this state (or country) and students who were not; and student eye colors. Students identify the fraction and an approximate percent for each portion of the data and make a circle graph for each data set.

Session 2 Follow-Up

Continued Work   Students continue to work on their surveys.

 **Homework**

Interpreting Percents

Materials

- Student Sheet 27 (1 per student)
- Student Sheet 28 (1 per student)
- Students' Survey Plans (from Session 1)

What Happens

In Choice Time, students work on three activities: they match given data to unlabeled circle graphs; they decide whether certain statements about percents are possible or impossible; and they begin preparing reports on their survey results. Their work focuses on:

- interpreting circle graphs
- matching circle graphs with data statements
- interpreting everyday situations that involve percents
- compiling and organizing survey results

Activity

Choice Time: Interpreting Percents

Three Choices During Sessions 3 and 4, students will have Choice Time. They will work at their seats and may do the three activities in any order. They may work alone or with others, but if they work alone, encourage them to discuss their results with classmates. Distribute the student sheets as you briefly introduce the activities. Questions to consider while you observe students at work are listed with each activity description.

Choice 1: Matching Data to Circle Graphs

On Student Sheet 27, Matching Data to Circle Graphs, students read three descriptions of data given in fractions, percents, and whole numbers, and match the statements with three of four unlabeled circle graphs, adding appropriate titles and labels. They also write their own description of data that matches the extra graph. They choose one graph and, on the back of the sheet, explain how they know it fits the data.

As students work, watch for these things: How do they identify the sentence that matches each graph? Do they use logical reasoning? How do they identify the segments on each circle graph? For example, do they use tools, such as the Percentractor or clocks? Do students invent reasonable situations to go with the extra circle graph (graph B)?

Choice 2: Possible or Impossible?

On Student Sheet 28, Possible or Impossible? students interpret sentences using percents and explain why the situations are possible or impossible. They then write eight sentences of their own, four possible and four impossible. As necessary, clarify that a sentence is *possible* if it could be true; it is *impossible* if it doesn't make mathematical sense.

As you observe students working on this activity: Are they able to make sense of the different situations? Do they discuss different interpretations with others? What kinds of possible/impossible sentences do they write? See the **Teacher Note,** Possible or Impossible? (p. 117), for comments on the four sentences students are considering.

Choice 3: Survey Reports

Meet briefly with each group to monitor their progress in collecting their survey data and preparing their reports. Have the students begun their data collection? Are they encountering any difficulties? Do they need to revise or add to their plans? Are they able to show their results clearly as raw data? Are they able to represent the raw data as fractions and percents? Do their circle graphs accurately represent their data? Are they able to draw any conclusions from their results?

Name _____ Date _____

Matching Data to Circle Graphs

Which circle graph goes with each set of data? Label the graphs. Give them titles. Write a sentence that matches the extra graph.

1. In a survey of favorite games, $\frac{2}{3}$ liked team games, $\frac{1}{6}$ liked board games, and $\frac{1}{6}$ liked individual games.

2. In a dog food test, 75% of the dogs ran to a bowl of Meato, while only $12\frac{1}{2}$% of the dogs chose Brand X and $12\frac{1}{2}$% chose Brand Z.

3. In a fifth grade class, 14 students walk to school, 6 students ride bikes, and 4 students come by car.

4. ___100 people came to my party. 50 of them drank soda and ate chips. 25 ate chips but no soda. 25 didn't eat or drink at all.___

Now choose one graph. Explain how you know the data fit that graph.

Discussing the Choices

About 20 minutes before the end of Session 4, call the class together to discuss their work on the two student sheets.

For Student Sheet 27, Matching Data to Circle Graphs, ask several groups to share their strategies for finding which graph went with which sentence. Students may also share the sentences they wrote for the extra graph (graph B).

Allow plenty of time to cover Student Sheet 28, Possible or Impossible? Discuss the sentences in pairs: What is the difference between almost identical sentences? How do "small" differences affect the situations? What reasons do students give for deciding whether a sentence is possible or impossible? After you have discussed all four sentences, students read examples of possible/impossible sentences they wrote. Their classmates decide whether the sentences are possible or impossible. If your class is large, students might do this last activity in small groups.

Sessions 3 and 4 Follow-Up

🏠 **Homework**

More Survey Work   Students continue to work on their surveys. Remind them that they must have all the data with them in the next session so they can prepare the final reports.

Possible or Impossible?

Making sense of the four sentences on Student Sheet 28, Possible or Impossible? can be difficult for students. While it is fairly easy for students to comprehend the notion of a whole being equal to 100 percent, the sentences on this student sheet bring up some more subtle issues.

Sentence 1. In one class, 47% of the students are girls, and 57% of the students are boys.

This sentence is easiest for students to interpret. Throughout the unit, they have been thinking of 100 percent as the whole, and combinations of percents must total 100.

Sentence 2. In one class, 47% of the students are girls, and 57% of the students walk to school.

This sentence is more difficult to interpret. Some students will observe, "It's possible, because some of the girls can also walk." However, others will add 47 percent and 57 percent and decide that the sentence is impossible because the percents add to more than 100. While 47 percent and 57 percent are parts of the same whole, the whole class has been divided into two unrelated and probably overlapping subgroups—gender and mode of transportation to school.

If your students have difficulty understanding sentence 2, you might ask students who are girls to go to one side of the room. Find the percent (or fraction) of the class that is girls. After the girls sit down, ask students who walk to school to go to the other side of the room. Find the percent (or fraction) of the class that walks to school. Do the percents (fractions) add to 100 (1)? Discuss why the percents (or fractions) turned out the way they did, and why it doesn't make sense to combine unrelated and overlapping subgroups.

Sentence 3. On Friday, 200% of the students were wearing red.

For some students this sentence will be obviously impossible. They will say things like, "It can only be 100 percent. Even if you add more people, they will be worth less." They know that 100 percent is the whole and you can't have more than the whole. Other students might suggest, "It's possible because it could be two classes." It is difficult for some students to realize that once a group is identified, even though it may not be clearly specified, you can't have more than 100 percent.

If some students are confused, you might ask them to identify a subgroup of the class, such as the boys. Then ask, "Is it possible for 200 percent of the boys in the class to like pizza?" If they say yes, because they're thinking of the boys in two classes, point out that they have changed the group, so you must now restate the question. "OK, now our group is the boys in our room and in Mrs. Alvarado's room. Can 200 percent of the boys in these two classrooms like pizza?"

Sentence 4. On Friday, 100% of the students were wearing red.

This one will be obvious to most students. If some believe this sentence is impossible, other students can give examples showing why it is possible. For example, "It's possible because the students all planned to wear red," or "It was red day." You might discuss the difference between *highly unlikely* and *impossible*.

Survey Reports

Materials

- Circle Graphs (1 per group, optional)
- Students' Percentractors (from Session 2)
- Large paper (1 per group)
- Colored pencils, crayons, or markers
- Glue
- Scissors
- Large stick-on notes (several per student)

What Happens

Students finish preparing their survey reports, showing the results for each of three questions as familiar fractions, as percents, and in circle graphs. Groups share their reports with the class by posting them for others to review and by orally sharing a few of their conclusions. Their work focuses on:

- compiling and organizing survey results
- representing raw data using familiar fractions and percents
- representing data from two subgroups in circle graphs
- communicating about survey findings

Activity

Preparing Final Reports

Discuss and post a list of the components of the final report (shown on the bottom of Student Sheet 26, Survey Plans):

1. The three hypotheses you investigated, and the percent of each group you predicted for each hypothesis.

2. A description of how your group collected the data. Include specifics such as the names and locations of places you went, and when and for how long you collected data.

3. The results of your three surveys. For each hypothesis, report your results in three ways:

   - raw data; tell the total number of people you surveyed and how many were from each group
   - actual fractions and familiar fractions; for example, maybe 21/62 (actual) or about 1/3 (familiar) were adults
   - percents of each group who participate

4. Three circle graphs, one for each hypothesis, to display your results.

5. One or two paragraphs stating your conclusions. What general interpretations do you make of your findings? Did your results match your hypotheses? Do you have any new hypotheses? Do you think you would get the same results if you repeated your survey? Why or why not? What would you do differently if you did the survey again?

Students meet in their small groups to discuss their results and to convert their raw data to familiar fractions and percents. They may want to divide the tasks for the report preparation, perhaps having two students prepare the graphs while the other two prepare the written comparisons. Provide larger paper, such as 11-by-17-inch copier paper or colored construction paper, for data displays. Students can use circle graphs cut from the Circle Graphs sheet, or make their own graphs (perhaps by tracing around a Percentractor).

Sharing the Reports

Students post their reports and circulate around the room to observe one another's work. They write any questions or comments about particular reports on stick-on notes that they attach to the report. Comments should focus primarily on the content of the reports, rather than on issues of form, such as neatness or spelling. To help students frame their questions or comments, you might suggest that students consider the following:

- Is it clear what hypotheses the group was investigating?
- Do you understand how and where students collected the data?
- Are the results presented in a clear way and related to the hypotheses?

When everybody has had a chance to see the reports, each group of students shares with the class one or two conclusions about their findings. They also address questions or comments received on the stick-on notes.

After students have shared their group findings, hold a brief discussion about the findings more generally.

How did your findings match your predictions? What surprised you? What did you learn that interested you? Are there any results that you think need further research? Why?

Assessment

Evaluating the Final Reports

You can assess students' learning during this unit by examining their survey plans (Student Sheet 26) and their final reports, as well as the comments and questions they make about other students' displays. Following are some questions to consider as you review students' work.

- Did the students make a reasonable plan? Did they identify three hypotheses and describe reasonable and feasible ways to collect data on a sample group?

- Were the students able to follow their plan? Do their reports include information about any deviations from the plan?

- Do students report their results clearly? Is it clear, for example, what the numbers reported as raw data represent?

- Are students able to convert their raw data to familiar fractions and percents for all three hypotheses?

- Are students able to represent their results in circle graphs? Can you easily tell from their displays the differences in percents of each of the two groups?

- Do students' written conclusions match their data? Do they recognize any limitations to their conclusions, such as a short amount of time spent collecting data?

- Do they have ideas about what they would change? Have they developed new hypotheses or questions?

- Are students able to make observations and ask questions about other students' work? Do they notice the relationships between results and the methods used for collecting data?

Two Days in My Life

What Happens

Students describe a typical day in their life today (as children) and as they imagine their life will be at age 30 (as adults). They classify their daily activities into categories and determine the number of hours and the fraction and percent of the day for each category. They make circle graphs to show the results. Their work focuses on:

- organizing and categorizing data
- representing data as fractions and percents
- representing data in circle graphs

Materials

- Student Sheet 29 (1 per student)
- Student Sheet 30 (1 per student)

Activity

A Typical Day

In this activity, students consider from a personal perspective how age differences affect participation in various activities. That is, they compare how they spend their time today (as children) with how they think they will spend it when they are 30 years old (as adults). Introduce the first part of the activity.

Think about a typical day for you—maybe one like today, when you are in school. What fraction of the day do you think you spend in school? What fraction of the day do you spend sleeping?

Provide time for students to think about and respond to these questions. Students share and compare their answers and how they arrived at them.

What other things do you do during a typical day?

Write responses on the board as students share what they do. Students will have many things in common, such as eating and getting dressed. There will be some activities that vary in either content or time typically spent; for example, playing sports, doing homework and chores, playing a musical instrument, watching TV.

Encourage students to group the things they do into a few major categories.

We do many different things during a day. Let's group what you typically do into no more than five categories. What could those categories be?

Thinking about their own lives, students suggest categories that would work. Record their ideas on the board. If there is enough in common among the categories, your whole class (or certain groups of students) may decide to use the same categories. Some categories that students commonly suggest are eating, sleeping, school, sports, homework and chores, watching TV, practicing an instrument, and going out.

Next, ask students to think about what a typical day will be like when they are 30 years old, and listen to a few of their ideas.

You know what a typical day is like for you now. Can you think of what a typical day might be like when you're 30 years old? What things that you do will be the same? What will be different?

Distribute Student Sheet 29, Typical Daily Schedules. Explain that on this sheet, students are to describe two typical days—one that represents their life today, and another one as they think life will be when they are 30. When they have finished, they should group each set of daily activities into no more than five different categories, which they list. Their categories for today and for age 30, however, do not need to be the same.

Representing Typical Days Distribute Student Sheet 30, Two Typical Days in My Life. Using information from their Typical Daily Schedules, students complete the tables and make circle graphs to show a typical day at the two different ages. When they finish the sheet, students write a short report comparing the two days using fractions and percents.

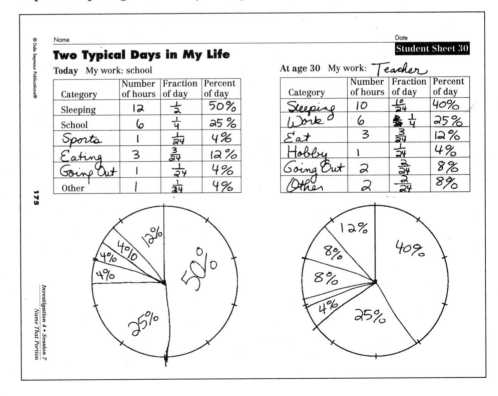

Observing the Students   Consider these questions as you observe students at work and when you look at their work:

■ Are students' descriptions of a typical day realistic? Are the time allocations reasonable?

■ Are students able to classify their daily activities into no more than five categories? Do they choose categories that represent significant amounts of time and the most important activities in their daily schedule?

■ Do students make sensible interpretations of the numbers? For example, do the hours in a typical day add to 24? the percents to 100? What methods do students use to convert between hours, fractions of the day, and percents?

■ What methods do students use to make their circle graphs? Do they approximate or eyeball where to draw the dividing lines? Do they use the marks around the circumference? Do they use their Percentractor? Do their representations on the circle graph roughly approximate their data in the table?

Activity

Choosing Student Work to Save

As the unit ends, you may want to use one of the following options for creating a record of students' work on this unit.

■ Students look back through their folders or notebooks and write about what they learned in this unit, what they remember most, and what was hard or easy for them. Students could do this during their writing time.

■ Students select one to two pieces of their work as their best work, and you also choose one to two pieces, to be saved in a portfolio for the year. You might include students' final projects, including the reports and circle graphs (use photocopies of the final reports). Students can create a separate page with brief comments describing each piece of work.

■ You may want to send a selection of work home for families to see. Students write a cover letter describing their work in this unit. This work should be returned if you are keeping year-long portfolios.

Seeing Numbers

Basic Activity

Students are shown a number of objects arranged in a configuration that makes the number easy to recognize. They find different ways to describe number relationships apparent in the arrangement. Then, they rearrange the objects to represent other number relationships, and they find different ways to describe those relationships.

As students work on this activity, they build their understanding of number relationships such as factors, multiples, fractions of a whole, and partitions. They explore different ways of describing these relationships, including fraction notation, factor pairs, and equations. Their work focuses on:

- exploring number relationships such as factors and fractions of a whole

- developing a visual model for factors, fractions, and partitions of a whole number

- finding different ways to describe number relationships, including fraction notation, factor pairs, and equations

Materials

- Overhead projector

- Small objects such as counting chips, blocks, tiles, buttons, or pennies, 30–40 of one kind

- Loops of string to surround areas on the overhead projector, each about 12 inches in circumference

- Small objects of a variety of shapes (for Fractions variation)

Procedure

Before turning on the overhead projector, arrange a composite number of chips on the overhead in an array or other grouping so that the number is easy to recognize. Introduce the activity with a number such as 15 that has only a few factors. For 15, you might lay out a 3 by 5 array. For 25, you might arrange 5 clumps of 5. For 24, you might lay out groups of 3 in 2 rows of 4.

Step 1. Show the arrangement for 5 seconds.
Then cover it.

Step 2. Students tell their partners what they saw.
Students may need to draw what they remember. Do they remember how the chips are arranged? Do they know how many chips there are in all?

Step 3. Display the arrangement again.
This time leave the arrangement visible while students share how they see it. They tell how many objects there are and how they figured out the number. Ask if anyone figured it out a different way.

Step 4. Students write down some number relationships they see in the display.
You might ask questions like these to get them started: "What can you see in this display about 24 (the total number)? What factor pairs do you see? In this arrangement, what numbers divide 24 evenly? What fractions of 24 can you see? Talk with your partners about what you notice and what in the display makes you think of this."

Step 5. List student responses.
As students describe the number relationships they see, write their statements as sentences and as equations. Confirm with students that you are writing what they mean. Invite students to show how they are grouping the objects, or demonstrate it using a loop of string. For 24, their ideas might include statements like these:

- One-eighth of twenty-four is three; there are eight groups of three beans. You can see it in this way:

$$\frac{1}{8} \text{ of } 24 = 3$$

■ Two-eighths of twenty-four is six; that's two groups of three.

$\frac{2}{8}$ of 24 = 6

■ Eight groups of three make twenty-four.

$8 \times 3 = 24$

■ Four times three plus four times three makes twenty-four. If you put one loop around the top line and the other around the bottom line you have twelve in each; twelve and twelve are twenty-four.

$(4 \times 3) + (4 \times 3) = 24$

■ Two times four times three is twenty-four; two rows, four groups in each row, three things in a group.

$2 \times 4 \times 3 = 24$

Step 6. Ask students to suggest another arrangement of the same total to show different number relationships. "How else might you arrange these objects to show different number relationships? to show different factors? What other fractions of 24 can we show?" For example, students might suggest a grouping that highlights the factors 6 and 4, and fractions that are sixths.

○○ ○○ ○○ ○○ ○○ ○○
○○ ○○ ○○ ○○ ○○ ○○

Variations

Large Numbers Make arrangements for large numbers by writing numbers on the overhead instead of placing objects. For example, you might write one of these arrangements for 200:

4×10 $\qquad$ 4×10

$\qquad$ 4×10

4×10 $\qquad$ 4×10

20 20 20 20 20
20 20 20 20 20

Number Sentences For either an arrangement of objects or an arrangement of numbers (as in the Large Number variation), you might focus the activity on writing equations and other notations for computation. Working alone or in pairs, students generate as many number statements as they can about the arrangement you are showing. Pool all the different statements, perhaps by asking each pair to each write one of their equations on the board. Here are some possibilities for the arrangement of 24 chips in 3 groups of 8:

$\frac{24}{8} = 3$ $\qquad$ $\frac{1}{8}$ of 24 = 3 $\qquad$ $\frac{2}{8}$ of 24 = 6

$12 \times \frac{1}{4} = 3$ $\qquad$ $\frac{3}{4} \times 12 = 9$ $\qquad$ $24 \div 3 = 8$

$3 \times 8 = 24$ $\qquad$ $12 + 12 = 24$

$\begin{array}{r} 4 \\ \times\ 3 \\ \hline 12 \end{array}$ $\qquad$ $3 + 3 + 3 + 3 = 12$ $\qquad$ $8\overline{)24}^{\,3}$

Fractions of Different Shapes (and Colors)
Put a mixture of 5–10 small objects on the overhead. You might use a combination of paper clips, erasers, pattern blocks, counting chips, magnetic letters or numbers, and plastic objects in familiar shapes (animals, trees, house, people, boats, cars, and so forth). Include transparent shapes in colors if you have some. Ask students to make statements about parts of the whole. Start with "___ out of ___" statements and later ask for fraction statements. For example:

■ 3 out of 7 are paper clips; 3/7 of the objects are paper clips.

■ 2 out of 7 are round; 2/7 of the objects are round.

"Show and Tell" Numbers Assign students a particular number. "How can you show [the number]? What can you say about [the number]?" Students draw one or more arrangements of objects for that number and write as many statements as they can that describe the number relationships related to each arrangement.

Exploring Data

Basic Activity

You or the students decide on something to observe about themselves. Because this is a Ten-Minute Math activity, the data they collect must be something they already know or can observe easily around them. Once the question is determined, quickly organize the data as students give individual answers to the question. The data can be organized as a line plot, a list, a table, or a bar graph. Then students describe what they can tell from the data, generate some new questions, and, if appropriate, make predictions about what will happen the next time they collect the same data.

Exploring Data is designed to give students many quick opportunities to collect, graph, describe, and interpret data about themselves and the world around them. Students focus on:

- describing important features of the data
- interpreting and posing questions about the data

Procedure

Step 1. Choose a question. Make sure the question involves data that students know or can observe: How many buttons are you wearing today? What month is your birthday? What is the best thing you ate yesterday? Are you wearing shoes or sneakers or sandals? How did you get to school today?

Step 2. Quickly collect and display the data. Use a list, a table, a line plot, or a bar graph. For example, a line plot for data about how many buttons students are wearing could look something like this:

```
        X
X       X       X
X       X       X
X       X   X   X   X
X       X   X   X   X
X   X   X   X   X   X       X
0   1   2   3   4   5   6
```

Number of Buttons

Step 3. Ask students to describe the data. What do they notice about their data? For data that have a numerical order (How many buttons do you have today? How many people live in your house? How many months until your birthday?), ask questions like these: "Are the data spread out or close together? What is the highest and lowest value? Where do most of the data seem to fall? What seems typical or usual for this class?"

For data in categories (What is your favorite book? How do you get to school? What month is your birthday?), ask questions like these: "Which categories have a lot of data? few data? none? Is there a way to categorize the data differently to get other information?"

Step 4. Ask students to interpret and predict. "Why do you think that the data came out this way? Does anything about the data surprise you? Do you think we'd get similar data if we collected it tomorrow? next week? in another class? with adults?"

Step 5. List any new questions. Keep a running list of questions you can use for further data collection and analysis. You may want to ask some of these questions again.

Variations

Data from Home Students might collect data about routines at home: What time do your brothers and sisters go to bed? What do you usually eat for breakfast?

Data from Another Class or Other Teachers Depending on your school situation, you may be able to assign students to collect data from other classrooms or other teachers. Students are always interested in surveying others about questions that interest them, such as this one: When you were little, what did you like best about school? What grade did you like the best?

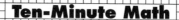
Categories If students take surveys about "favorites"—flavor of ice cream, breakfast cereal, book, color—or other data that falls into categories, the graphs are often flat and uninteresting. There is not too much to say, for example, about a graph like this:

```
X
X       X               X       X
X       X       X       X       X       X
X       X       X       X       X       X
```
| vanilla | chocolate | straw-berry | chocolate chip | Rocky Road | vanilla fudge |

It is more interesting for students to group their results into fewer, more descriptive categories, so that they can see other things about the data. In this case, even though vanilla seems to be the favorite in the graph above, another way of grouping the data seems to show that flavors with some chocolate in them are really the favorites.

Chocolate flavors   //// //// /

Flavors without chocolate   //// /

Familiar Fractions Once data is grouped into two or three categories, students express the data as fractions and then find familiar fractions and percents to describe the amounts. For example, in the ice cream choices survey, 6/17 prefer flavors without chocolate. This is less than half. It is about a third since 6/18 is a third. Seventeenths are larger than eighteenths, so it's more than 33⅓%, maybe about 35%. Students can check by dividing 6 by 17 on the calculator.

The following activities will help ensure that this unit is comprehensible to students who are acquiring English as a second language. The suggested approach is based on *The Natural Approach: Language Acquisition in the Classroom* by Stephen D. Krashen and Tracy D. Terrell (Alemany Press, 1983). The intent is for second-language learners to acquire new vocabulary in an active, meaningful context.

Note that *acquiring* a word is different from *learning* a word. Depending on their level of proficiency, students may be able to comprehend a word upon hearing it during an investigation, without being able to say it. Other students may be able to use the word orally, but not read or write it. The goal is to help students naturally acquire targeted vocabulary at their present level of proficiency.

We suggest using these activities just before the related investigations. The activities can also be led by English-proficient students.

Investigation 2
halfway, larger, smaller

1. Draw a straight, horizontal line on the board with a dot at each end. Label the dots with names of cities familiar to your students. Draw a short mark to divide the line in half, and explain that this point is *halfway* between the two cities.

2. Draw several similar lines of different lengths. For each line, ask volunteers to mark the point that is about *halfway* between the two cities.

3. Write a number along each line to identify the distance between cities in miles or kilometers. Point to different pairs of lines and ask students to identify the *larger* distance and the *smaller* distance.

4. Ask the students to estimate a point halfway across the classroom, and halfway across the board.

5. Give directions that change upon reaching the halfway point. For example:

   Take small steps until you get halfway across the room. Then take larger steps.

   Draw a row of large circles until you get halfway across the board. Then draw smaller circles.

Investigation 4
male, female, children, adults

1. Show several photographs or illustrations of people of different ages (you might use magazines or textbooks). Identify the people by age and gender as you point. For example:

   There are two *males* and three *females* in this picture. One male and one female are *adults*. These other three people are *children*.

2. Ask the students to each draw a simple sketch of their family. Ask them to look at their pictures as they answer questions with one-word responses.

   Whose family has the most adults?

   How many children are in Antonio's family?

   Are there more males or more females in Mei-Ling's family?

Blackline Masters

Family Letter   131

Dear Family,

In mathematics, our class is starting a unit called *Name That Portion.* We will be studying three different ways to talk about numbers less than 1: fractions (1/4), percents (25%), and decimals (0.25). This unit emphasizes similarities and connections among these ideas. Students come to see percents, fractions, and decimals as different ways to represent the same number.

Knowledge of these relationships helps students estimate answers to problems and catch computational errors, because they know what to expect about the size of a number. To help students develop strategies to solve problems using fractions, decimals, and percents, we will use visual models like these:

10-by-10 grids
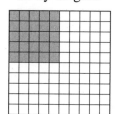

clock faces
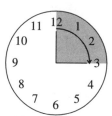

paper strips

- When your child brings home Completed Percent Equivalent Strips, consider posting one in the kitchen or living room. When fractions or percents come up in conversation, consult the Strip to find the equivalent value.

- From time to time, your child will bring home a number game to play with family members. Please sit down and play these games with your child. All the games involve strategy, as well as work with fractions, percents, or decimals.

- Later in the unit, groups of children may be conducting optional observational surveys. A few surveys may involve going to public places, such as stores. Plan to talk with your child and with me about this survey and determine appropriate places outside the home where your child might go with a classmate.

As in other *Investigations* units, we encourage students to develop several strategies that make sense to them for solving fraction, percent, and decimal problems. When you see your child using a strategy that is not familiar to you, ask for an explanation. The conversation will be educational for both you and your child.

Sincerely,

What Do You Already Know? (page 1 of 2)

1. **a.** In one group, 2 out of 5 students are wearing glasses. What fraction is that?

    b. What fraction of the 5 students are not wearing glasses?

2. **a.** Park cut his small pizza into sixths. He ate the whole pizza. How many pieces did he eat?

    b. Jen cut her pizza into eighths. She ate half of the pieces. How many pieces did she eat?

3. In one class, $\frac{1}{6}$ of the students raked leaves while the rest picked up trash on the playground. What fraction of the students picked up trash?

4. **a.** How much money is $\frac{1}{4}$ of a dollar? Write it with a decimal point.

    b. How much money is $\frac{3}{4}$ of a dollar? Write it with a decimal point.

5. Chad, Evan, and Gene were the first to finish a swimming race. Chad swam the race in 2 minutes 5.96 seconds. Evan's time was 2 minutes 10.01 seconds. Gene's time was 2 minutes 7.25 seconds. Who won the race?

6. **a.** A spelling pretest had 14 words. Dana spelled 100% of them correctly. How many words did she spell correctly?

    b. Cassie spelled only 7 out of the 14 words correctly. What percent of the words did she spell correctly?

What Do You Already Know? (page 2 of 2)

7. **a.** Jonas wins $\frac{1}{3}$ of these marbles.

    Draw a circle around them.

    b. Ping wins $\frac{2}{3}$ of the marbles.

    How many marbles does she win?

8. It rained 0.25 inches yesterday. How do you show that amount as a fraction of an inch?

9. **a.** When 8 children go on a picnic, $\frac{6}{8}$ of them wear jeans. How many wear jeans?

    b. What fraction do not wear jeans?

10. **a.** If 100% of your class likes carrots, how many students like carrots?

    b. If 50% of your class likes peas, how many students like peas?

Everyday Uses of Fractions, Decimals, and Percents

List in the spaces below the everyday uses you find for fractions, decimals, and percents. Cut out your examples from old magazines and newspapers, and attach them to this sheet.

Everyday Uses of Fractions

Everyday Uses of Decimals

Everyday Uses of Percents

Remember to bring this sheet to school so we can add your examples to the class list.

Grid Patterns

Grid 1

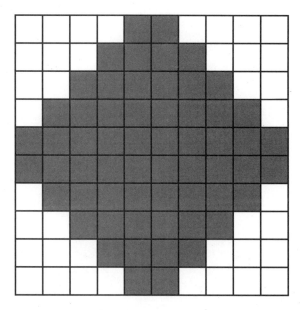

What portion is shaded?

Percent:

Fractions:

Grid 2

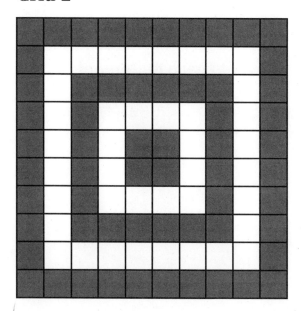

What portion is shaded?

Percent:

Fractions:

Grid 3

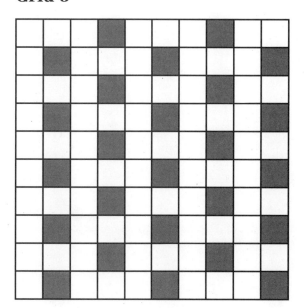

What portion is shaded?

Percent:

Fractions:

Grid 4

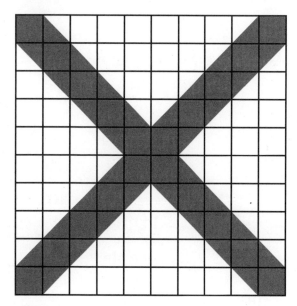

What portion is shaded?

Percent:

Fractions:

What Fraction Do You See?

Just as we have done in class, write statements about a small group of people, family members or friends. Draw the group and the characteristic you described and record the fraction that represents each statement.

This is the group I am describing:

1. _____ out of _____ people _____

2. _____ out of _____ people _____

3. _____ out of _____ people _____

4. _____ out of _____ people _____

Fraction and Percent Equivalents

$\frac{1}{2} =$	$\frac{1}{3} =$	$\frac{1}{4} =$	$\frac{1}{5} =$	$\frac{1}{6} =$	$\frac{1}{8} =$	$\frac{1}{10} =$
$\frac{2}{2} = 100\%$	$\frac{2}{3} =$	$\frac{2}{4} =$	$\frac{2}{5} =$	$\frac{2}{6} =$	$\frac{2}{8} =$	$\frac{2}{10} =$
	$\frac{3}{3} = 100\%$	$\frac{3}{4} =$	$\frac{3}{5} =$	$\frac{3}{6} =$	$\frac{3}{8} =$	$\frac{3}{10} =$
		$\frac{4}{4} = 100\%$	$\frac{4}{5} =$	$\frac{4}{6} =$	$\frac{4}{8} =$	$\frac{4}{10} =$
			$\frac{5}{5} = 100\%$	$\frac{5}{6} =$	$\frac{5}{8} =$	$\frac{5}{10} =$
				$\frac{6}{6} = 100\%$	$\frac{6}{8} =$	$\frac{6}{10} =$
					$\frac{7}{8} =$	$\frac{7}{10} =$
					$\frac{8}{8} = 100\%$	$\frac{8}{10} =$
						$\frac{9}{10} =$
						$\frac{10}{10} = 100\%$

Seeing Fractions and Percents on Grids

For each grid below, choose a fraction and color in the portion of the grid that represents the fraction. Write the fraction and the percent equivalent for each.

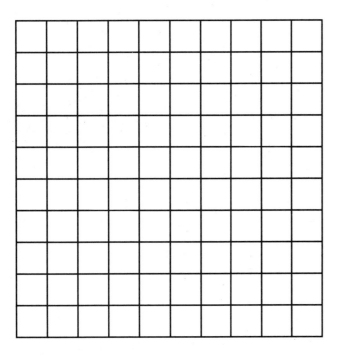

$$\underline{\hspace{1cm}} = \frac{\underline{\hspace{1cm}}}{100} = \underline{\hspace{1cm}}\%$$

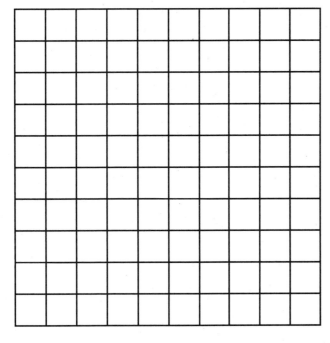

$$\underline{\hspace{1cm}} = \frac{\underline{\hspace{1cm}}}{100} = \underline{\hspace{1cm}}\%$$

© Dale Seymour Publications®

Grouping Equivalent Fractions

Record all the fractions you can that are equal to the percent listed.

For example: $50\% = \frac{1}{2} = \frac{2}{4} = \frac{3}{6} = \frac{4}{8} = \frac{5}{10}$

1. $33\frac{1}{3}\% =$

2. $25\% =$

3. $40\% =$

4. $75\% =$

5. $80\% =$

Remember to bring this sheet back to class so you can add these examples to your Equivalents sheet.

How to Play the In-Between Game

Materials: Fraction Cards—diamond (♦) cards only, Completed Percent
             Equivalents Strip (for reference only)

Players: 2

1. Place the 10%, 50%, and 90% cards on the table (see picture).

2. Mix the Fraction Cards. Deal six to each player.

3. Players take turns placing a card so it touches another card.
   You may place a card to the right of 10%, on either side of
   50%, to the left of 90%, or on top of any percent. As you play
   a card, state the fraction and its percent equivalent.

   For example, if you place the $\frac{1}{6}$ card to the right of 10%, you
   would say, "One-sixth is $16\frac{2}{3}$%."

4. Cards must be placed in increasing order, from left to right.

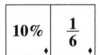   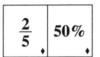

   A card may *not* be placed between two cards that are touching.

   In this example, the $\frac{1}{8}$ card may **not** be placed between the $\frac{1}{6}$ and
   the 10% cards. So, you can't place it in this round.

5. Your goal is to place as many cards as you can. The round is over
   when neither player can place any more cards. Your score is the
   number of cards left in your hand.

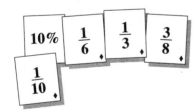      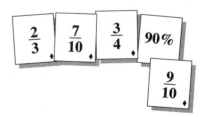

   At the end of a round, the table might look like this:

   Player 1 could not place $\frac{1}{8}$ and $\frac{4}{5}$ and so has a score of 2.
   Player 2 used all six cards and so has a score of 0.

6. At the end of five rounds, the player with the lowest score wins.

© Dale Seymour Publications®   **140**

Fraction and Percent Problems (page 1 of 2)

1. **a.** In a class of 40 students, 20 went to the computer lab yesterday. What percent went to the computer lab?

    b. At the same time, 10 out of the 40 students helped in the first grade class. What percent helped in the first grade?

    c. Five out of the 40 students worked at the writing center. What percent worked at the writing center?

    d. The rest of the students were absent. How many students were absent? What percent of the students were absent?

2. **a.** Name four different fractions that are between $\frac{1}{2}$ and 1 whole. Can you put them in order?

    b. Name some percents that are larger than 1 whole.

    c. Name some percents that are between $\frac{1}{4}$ and $\frac{1}{2}$.

3. Sonya and Adam have little loaves of bread that are the same size. Sonya cut hers into 8 equal slices and ate 3 of them. Adam cut his into 10 equal slices and ate 4.

    a. Whose pieces were bigger? How do you know?

    b. Who ate the most bread? How do you know?

4. **a.** If 25% of your class is jumping rope, about how many students are jumping rope?

    b. If 75% of your class is playing kickball, about how many students are playing kickball?

Fraction and Percent Problems (page 2 of 2)

5. **a.** For the first game of the season, 100 people came, and $\frac{1}{4}$ of them walked. How many people walked?

    b. For the second game of the season, 200 people came, and $\frac{1}{4}$ of them walked. How many people walked?

    c. What fraction of the 100 people did not walk? What fraction of the 200 people did not walk?

    d. How many of the 100 people did not walk? How many of the 200 people did not walk?

6. Rudy ate 25% of a pizza. Eli ate 50% of a different pizza. Is it possible that Rudy ate more pizza than Eli? Why do you think this?

$\frac{2}{3}$ and $\frac{3}{4}$

1. Write what you know about the fraction $\frac{2}{3}$. Write at least three statements.

2. Write what you know about the fraction $\frac{3}{4}$. Write at least three statements.

3. Write three reasons explaining how you know $\frac{3}{4}$ is larger than $\frac{2}{3}$.

PERCENT EQUIVALENTS STRIPS

Cut out four strips along heavy black lines. Each student marks the fractions on one strip.

| 10% | 20% | 30% | 40% | 50% | 60% | 70% | 80% | 90% |

| 10% | 20% | 30% | 40% | 50% | 60% | 70% | 80% | 90% |

| 10% | 20% | 30% | 40% | 50% | 60% | 70% | 80% | 90% |

| 10% | 20% | 30% | 40% | 50% | 60% | 70% | 80% | 90% |

© Dale Seymour Publications®

COMPLETED PERCENT EQUIVALENTS STRIPS

Cut out four strips along heavy black lines. Each group uses one to check their own strips.

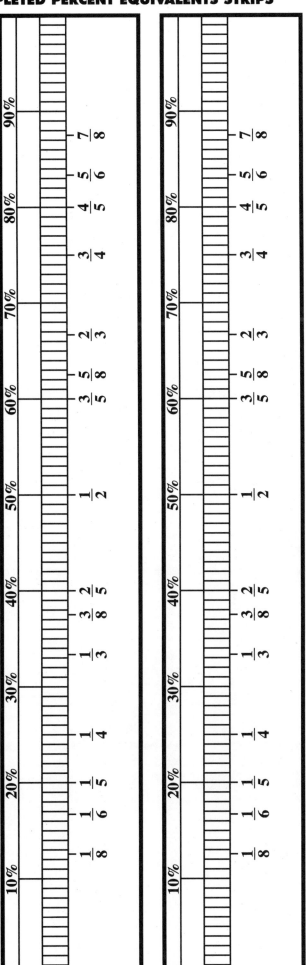

© Dale Seymour Publications®

$\dfrac{1}{2}$ ♦	$\dfrac{1}{3}$ ♦	$\dfrac{2}{3}$ ♦	$\dfrac{1}{4}$ ♦
$\dfrac{3}{4}$ ♦	$\dfrac{1}{5}$ ♦	$\dfrac{2}{5}$ ♦	$\dfrac{3}{5}$ ♦
$\dfrac{4}{5}$ ♦	$\dfrac{1}{6}$ ♦	$\dfrac{5}{6}$ ♦	$\dfrac{1}{8}$ ♦
$\dfrac{3}{8}$ ♦	$\dfrac{5}{8}$ ♦	$\dfrac{7}{8}$ ♦	$\dfrac{1}{10}$ ♦
$\dfrac{3}{10}$ ♦	$\dfrac{7}{10}$ ♦	$\dfrac{9}{10}$ ♦	50% ♦

Investigation 1 • Resource
Name That Portion

10% ◆	90% ◆	$\dfrac{2}{2}$	$\dfrac{3}{2}$
$\dfrac{3}{3}$	$\dfrac{4}{3}$	$\dfrac{2}{4}$	$\dfrac{4}{4}$
$\dfrac{5}{4}$	$\dfrac{6}{4}$	$\dfrac{5}{5}$	$\dfrac{6}{5}$
$\dfrac{7}{5}$	$\dfrac{2}{6}$	$\dfrac{3}{6}$	$\dfrac{4}{6}$
$\dfrac{6}{6}$	$\dfrac{7}{6}$	$\dfrac{8}{6}$	$\dfrac{9}{6}$

$\dfrac{2}{8}$	$\dfrac{4}{8}$	$\dfrac{6}{8}$	$\dfrac{8}{8}$
$\dfrac{9}{8}$	$\dfrac{10}{8}$	$\dfrac{11}{8}$	$\dfrac{12}{8}$
$\dfrac{2}{10}$	$\dfrac{4}{10}$	$\dfrac{5}{10}$	$\dfrac{6}{10}$
$\dfrac{8}{10}$	$\dfrac{10}{10}$	$\dfrac{11}{10}$	$\dfrac{12}{10}$
$\dfrac{13}{10}$	$\dfrac{14}{10}$	$\dfrac{15}{10}$	$\dfrac{1}{1}$

Investigation 1 • Resource
Name That Portion

© Dale Seymour Publications®

Clock Fractions

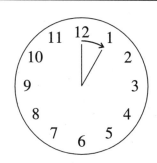 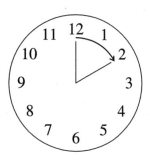 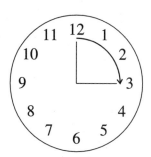

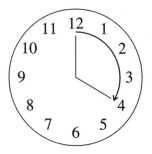 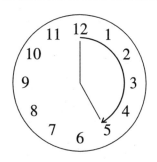 

  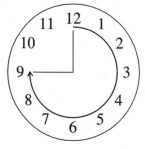

  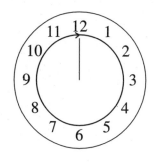

Clock Fractions Addition Problems

For each fraction addition problem you make up and solve, show your work on the clock face. Record your strategy for solving the problem.

1. ____ + ____ = ____

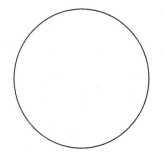

2. ____ + ____ = ____

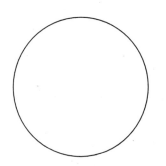

3. ____ + ____ = ____

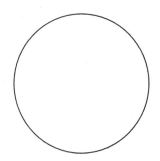

Fraction Strip Subtraction Problems

Using your fraction strips, make up and solve fraction
subtraction problems. Record the strategies you use in the
space below each problem.

1. _____ − _____ = _____

2. _____ − _____ = _____

3. _____ − _____ = _____

4. _____ − _____ = _____

How to Play Capture Fractions

Materials: Deck of Fraction Cards

Players: 2

How to Play:

1. Deal the cards evenly to each player. Players keep the cards face down in a pile.

2. In each round players turn their top card face up at the same time. The player with the larger fraction takes both cards and puts them on the bottom of his or her own pile.

3. If the cards show equivalent fractions, players turn over another card. The player with the larger fraction takes all four cards.

4. The player with the most cards wins. The game can be stopped at any time.

___

Record the fractions turned over in two of your rounds.
Explain how you figured out who won.

Player 1 turned over _____. Player 2 turned over _____.
Who won the round? How do you know?

Player 1 turned over _____. Player 2 turned over _____.
Who won the round? How do you know?

How to Play the Fraction Track Game

Materials: Fraction Cards, Fraction Track Gameboard
20 chips (or other small objects)

Players: 2–3, or 2 pairs

Playing to 1 (Introductory game)

1. Remove the percent cards and the 18 cards greater than 1 (such as $\frac{3}{2}$) from the deck. Fold under the right half of the Fraction Track Gameboard—only fractions from 0 to 1 should show.

2. Place seven chips on the gameboard, one on each track, at any fraction point less than $\frac{3}{4}$. Mix the cards and place the deck facedown.

3. Players take turns drawing the top card and moving a chip (or chips) to total the amount shown. You can move on one track or on several. For example, if the card is $\frac{3}{5}$, you can move $\frac{3}{5}$ on the fifths line, or $\frac{6}{10}$ on the tenths line, or a combination of moves on two or more lines, such as $\frac{1}{2}$ and $\frac{1}{10}$, or $\frac{1}{5}$ and $\frac{4}{10}$, or $\frac{1}{3}$, $\frac{1}{6}$, and $\frac{1}{10}$. The fraction on the card is the total that you move chips; it does not indicate points to land on.

4. The goal is to move chips so they land exactly on the number 1. When you land on 1, you win the chip. When a chip is won, place a new chip at 0 on the same track so the next player has a chip on every track. (This happens only when a player has completed a turn. You may not wrap around and keep going on the same track within a turn.)

Playing to 2 (Regular game)

The rules are the same as the introductory version, except:

1. Use all the Fraction Cards and the entire Fraction Track Gameboard.

2. The seven chips may be placed on any fractions less than $\frac{3}{2}$.

3. The goal is to move chips so they land exactly on the number 2.

More Everyday Uses of Fractions, Decimals, and Percents

Record or attach any examples of decimals you find. Explain the meaning of the decimals using equivalent fractions. If you can't find a decimal, you may substitute a fraction or percent.

1. _____

Equivalent:

2. _____

Equivalent:

Fractions of Pizza (page 1 of 2)

1. There are 12 children at a birthday party. There is enough pizza for each person to eat $\frac{3}{4}$ of a pizza. How many pizzas are there altogether?

2. Alyssa, Bianca, and Chase made their own pizzas. All three pizzas were the same size.

   a. Alyssa cut her pizza in half and ate 1 piece. What fraction of the pizza did she eat? What percent is that?

   b. Bianca cut her pizza into 8 pieces and ate 3 of them. What fraction of the pizza did she eat? What percent is that?

   c. Chase cut his pizza into 10 pieces and ate 4 of them. What fraction of the pizza did he eat? What percent is that?

   d. Who ate the most pizza? Who ate the least? How do you know?

3. Tito and Luis stuffed themselves with pizza. Tito ate $\frac{1}{4}$ of a cheese pizza, $\frac{3}{8}$ of a pepperoni pizza, and $\frac{1}{2}$ of a mushroom pizza. Luis ate $\frac{5}{8}$ of a cheese pizza and the other $\frac{1}{2}$ of the mushroom pizza. They want to know who ate more pizza. What can you tell them?

Fractions of Pizza (page 2 of 2)

4. Sanctora asked her little brother to help her make pizza for a neighbor. The neighbor paid Sanctora $12.00. She kept $\frac{3}{4}$ of the money and gave her brother the rest.

   a. What fraction did she give her brother?

   b. How much money did each of them get?

5. Today 500 people ate pizza in the school lunchroom. Of those, 25% were teachers and other adults. The rest were students at the school.

   a. What percent were students at the school?

   b. How many students ate pizza in the lunchroom?

6. We bought 5 pizzas for 10 people. One and $\frac{3}{8}$ pizza is left. How much did we eat? About how much did each person eat?

Moves on the Fraction Track

Record two moves that involved more than one track from the rounds of Fraction Track you played at home. Write your moves as addition problems.

For example: $\frac{7}{8} = \frac{1}{2} + \frac{3}{8}$

$\frac{3}{4} = \frac{2}{8} + \frac{1}{6} + \frac{1}{3}$

1. The fraction on my card was _____.

   This is how I moved:

2. The fraction on my card was _____.

   This is how I moved:

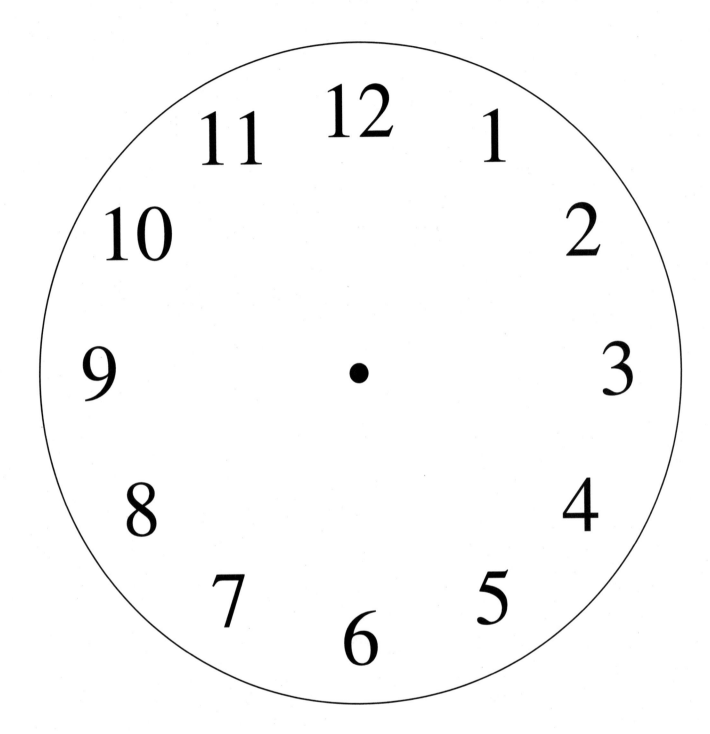

© Dale Seymour Publications®

FRACTION TRACK GAMEBOARD, SHEET 1

Tape together with Sheet 2 to make continuous tracks from 0 to 2. Overlap at the 1 dots.

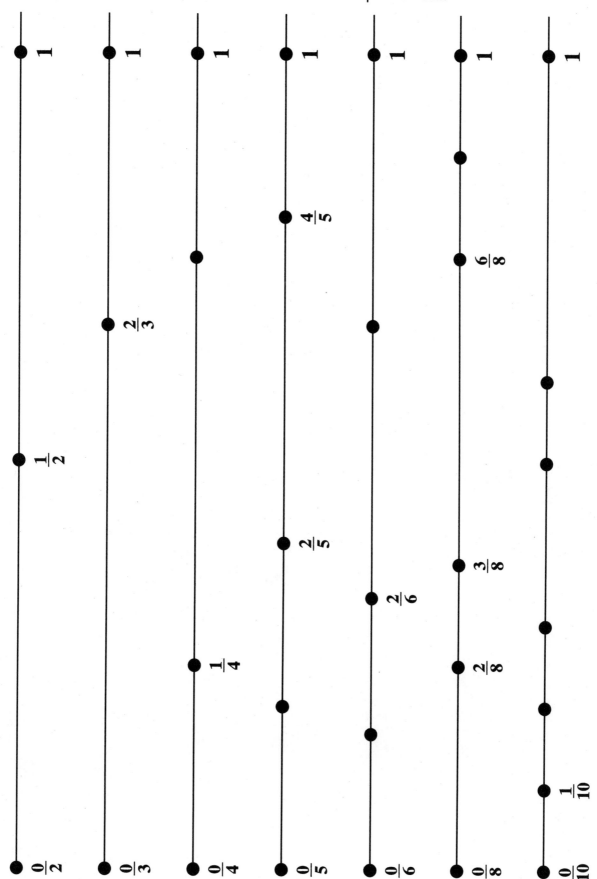

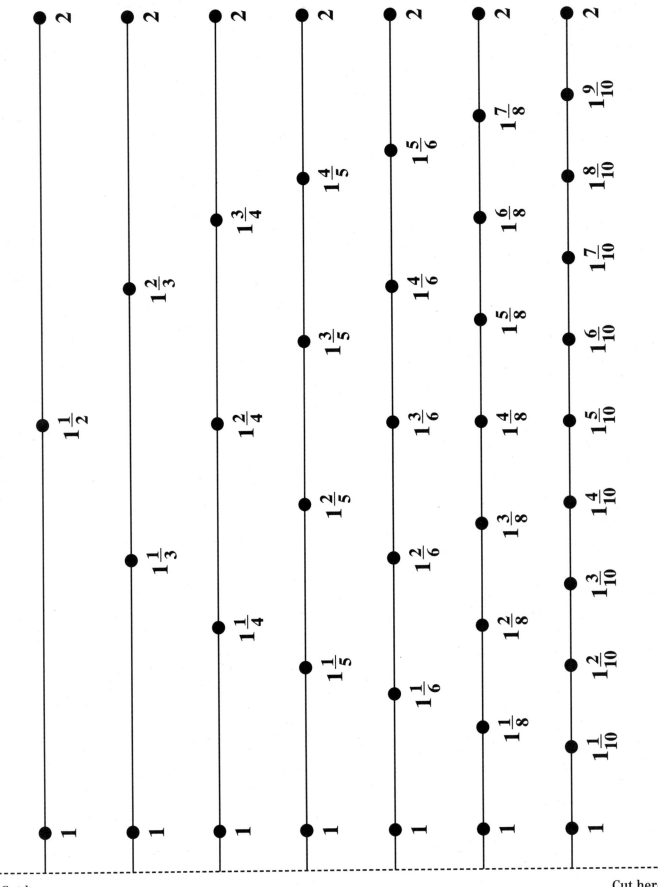

Cut here

Cut here

© Dale Seymour Publications®

How to Play Fill Two

Materials: One deck of Decimal Cards, Set A

Grids: 1 sheet per player

Crayons or markers (two or more colors) for each player

Players: 2

1. Mix the cards and turn the deck face down. Turn over the top four cards and place them face up in a row. After one of the four cards has been picked, replace it with the top card from the deck.

2. The goal is to shade in two of your grids as completely as possible.

3. Players take turns. On your turn, choose one of the face up cards, color in that amount on either grid, and write the decimal below the grid. You may never color in an amount that would more than fill a grid, and you may not split an amount to color in parts of two grids.

4. Change colors for each turn so that you can see the different decimals. As you write the decimal below the grid, use plus (+) signs between the decimals, making an equation that will show the total colored in on that grid.

5. If all cards showing are greater than the spaces left on your grids, you lose your turn until a card that you can use is turned up.

6. The game is over when neither player can choose a card. Players then find the total colored in on each grid and add them. The winner is the player whose final sum is closest to 2.

Variation: Fill Four

The rules for this game are the same as for Fill Two, except:

1. Use Decimal Cards Set A and Set B.

2. Each player fills four grids during a game. On a turn, you may color in the amount on any grid that has enough room.

3. The winner is the player whose final sum is closest to 4.

How to Play Smaller to Larger

Materials: Decimal Cards, Sets A and B. For 3 or 4 players, mix together two complete decks.

Players: 2, 3, or 4

1. Each player draws a 3-by-3 grid for a game mat, with spaces large enough for Decimal Cards to fit inside.

2. Mix the deck and place it face down between the players.

3. Players take turns. On your turn, draw the top card from the pile and decide where to place it on your game mat. The numbers must be in increasing order, from left to right in each row and from top to bottom in each column.

4. If you draw a card that you cannot place because of the numbers already on your game mat, you must keep the card in a pile and lose your turn.

Example:

Suppose after six turns your game mat looks like this. You draw 0.15 and it can't be played because 0.375 is already in the lowest place on the board. Put the 0.15 card in your pile of cards that could not be played.

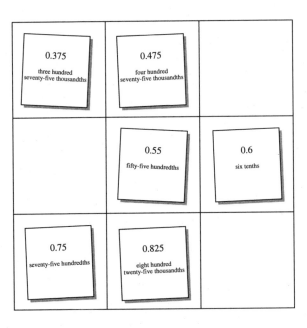

5. If you are unsure which of two numbers is larger, discuss them with other players.

6. The game is over when each player has filled all nine spaces.

7. The winner is the player who has the fewest cards that could not be played.

Fraction to Decimal Division Table

Numerator

N/D	1	2	3	4	5	6	7	8	9	10	11	12
1												
2												
3												
4												
5												
6												
7												
8												
9												
10												
11												
12												

Denominator

Fraction, Decimal, Percent Equivalents

Fraction	Decimal	Percent
	.33333 . . .	$33\frac{1}{3}\%$
$\frac{2}{3}$		
$5\frac{1}{4}$		
		250%

Fraction	Decimal	Percent
$\frac{1}{4}$		
		75%
$\frac{1}{8}$		
	0.375	

Scoring Sports and Other Problems

1. Michi has completed three events at a gymnastic meet. Her scores were 7.5, 8.1, and 8.5. She has one more event to go, the vault. She is hoping to get an overall score of 32 on all four events combined. What must her vault score be to give her a total score of 32?

2. In the same gymnastic meet, Jameel scored 8.8 on the floor event and 7.75 on the vault. How much better did he score on the floor?

3. A relay race is run. Each runner runs one leg, or $\frac{1}{8}$ kilometer. How many runners are required to run a total of $\frac{3}{4}$ kilometer?

4. **a.** What is $\frac{1}{4}$ of $13?

   b. What is $\frac{1}{4}$ of 13 feet of rope?

   c. How many cars are needed to take 13 children on a field trip if each car holds 4 children?

5. Ryan and Eva are talking about who is the better hitter in a baseball game. Ryan hit the ball 3 times out of 10 times at bat. Eva hit the ball 4 out of her 12 times at bat. Who is the better hitter in this game, and how do you know?

6. Lulani read that 39% of American homes own a dog. In her class of 30 students, 10 have dogs. Is this more than, less than, or the same as the national data Lulani read? How do you know?

Comparing Common Fractions

Use pictures, numbers, and/or words to find three ways to show that $\frac{2}{3}$ is larger than $\frac{2}{5}$.

More Fraction Comparisons

Choose two pairs from the following list. Use pictures, numbers, and/or words to find two ways to show which fraction is larger and how you know.

$\frac{1}{3}$ and $\frac{1}{4}$ $\frac{1}{2}$ and $\frac{3}{5}$ $\frac{5}{8}$ and $\frac{7}{10}$ $\frac{3}{2}$ and $\frac{4}{3}$

$\frac{9}{5}$ and $\frac{7}{4}$ $\frac{2}{3}$ and $\frac{5}{6}$ $\frac{1}{8}$ and $\frac{2}{10}$ $\frac{3}{4}$ and $\frac{4}{5}$

Pair 1: _____ and _____

1.

2.

Pair 2: _____ and _____

1.

2.

Tenths

Hundredths

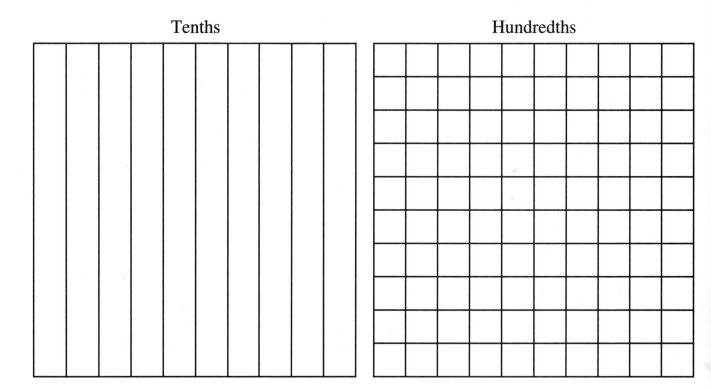

Thousandths

Ten-Thousandths

0.1	0.2	0.3	0.4
one-tenth	two-tenths	three-tenths	four-tenths
0.5	0.6	0.7	0.8
five-tenths	six-tenths	seven-tenths	eight-tenths
0.9	0.05	0.15	0.25
nine-tenths	five-hundredths	fifteen-hundredths	twenty-five hundredths
0.35	0.45	0.55	0.65
thirty-five hundredths	forty-five hundredths	fifty-five hundredths	sixty-five hundredths
0.75	0.85	0.95	
seventy-five hundredths	eighty-five hundredths	ninety-five hundredths	

0.025 twenty-five thousandths	**0.075** seventy-five thousandths	**0.125** one hundred twenty-five thousandths	**0.175** one hundred seventy-five thousandths
0.225 two hundred twenty-five thousandths	**0.275** two hundred seventy-five thousandths	**0.325** three hundred twenty-five thousandths	**0.375** three hundred seventy-five thousandths
0.425 four hundred twenty-five thousandths	**0.475** four hundred seventy-five thousandths	**0.525** five hundred twenty-five thousandths	**0.575** five hundred seventy-five thousandths
0.625 six hundred twenty-five thousandths	**0.675** six hundred seventy-five thousandths	**0.725** seven hundred twenty-five thousandths	**0.775** seven hundred seventy-five thousandths
0.825 eight hundred twenty-five thousandths	**0.875** eight hundred seventy-five thousandths	**0.925** nine hundred twenty-five thousandths	**0.975** nine hundred seventy-five thousandths

Survey Plans

1. Hypothesis: _____

    Predictions: _____   _____

            Group   Percent   Group   Percent

2. Hypothesis: _____

    Predictions: _____   _____

            Group   Percent   Group   Percent

3. Hypothesis: _____

    Predictions: _____   _____

            Group   Percent   Group   Percent

Describe your plan for conducting the investigation on the back of this sheet.

Final Report Checklist: Your final report should include the following:

☐ The three hypotheses you investigated, and your predictions for each.

☐ A description of how your group collected the data. Include places you went, and when and for how long you collected data.

☐ The results of your surveys. For each hypothesis, report your results in three ways:

- raw data: the total number surveyed, and how many from each group
- actual fractions and familiar (closely related) fractions
- actual percents of each group

☐ Three circle graphs, one for each hypothesis, to display your results.

☐ One or two paragraphs stating your conclusions. What general interpretations do you make of your findings? Did your results match your hypotheses? Do you have any new hypotheses? Do you think you would get the same results if you repeated your survey? Why or why not? What would you do differently if you did the survey again?

Matching Data to Circle Graphs

Which circle graph goes with each set of data? Label the graphs.
Give them titles. Write a sentence that matches the extra graph.

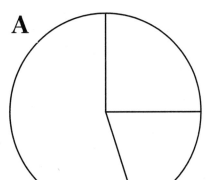

A

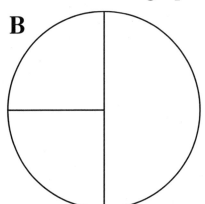

B

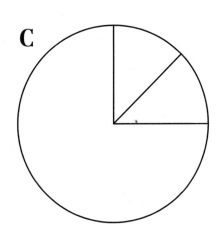

C

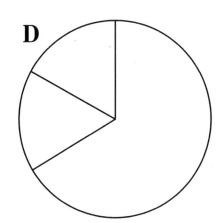

D

1. In a survey of favorite games, $\frac{2}{3}$ liked team games, $\frac{1}{6}$ liked board games, and $\frac{1}{6}$ liked individual games.

2. In a dog food test, 75% of the dogs ran to a bowl of Meato, while only $12\frac{1}{2}$% of the dogs chose Brand X and $12\frac{1}{2}$% chose Brand Z.

3. In a fifth grade class, 14 students walk to school, 6 students ride bikes, and 4 students come by car.

4. _____

   _____

   _____

Now choose one graph. Explain how you know the data fit that graph.

Investigation 4 • Sessions 3–4
Name That Portion

Possible or Impossible?

Which sentences are possible? Which are impossible?
Explain why. Then write four possible and four impossible
percent sentences on the back of the sheet.

1. In one class, 47% of the students are girls, and 57% of
the students are boys.

Possible or impossible? Why?

2. In one class, 47% of the students are girls, and 57% of
the students walk to school.

Possible or impossible? Why?

3. On Friday, 200% of the students were wearing red.

Possible or impossible? Why?

4. On Friday, 100% of the students were wearing red.

Possible or impossible? Why?

Typical Daily Schedules

Describe a typical day in your life today and what you think a typical day will be like when you are 30 years old. Include what you will be doing at different times during the 24 hours. Then group your activities into no more than five categories.

Today My work: school	**At age 30** My work: _____
Categories: sleeping school	**Categories:** sleeping

Two Typical Days in My Life

Today My work: school

Category	Number of hours	Fraction of day	Percent of day
Sleeping			
School			
Other			

At age 30 My work:

Category	Number of hours	Fraction of day	Percent of day

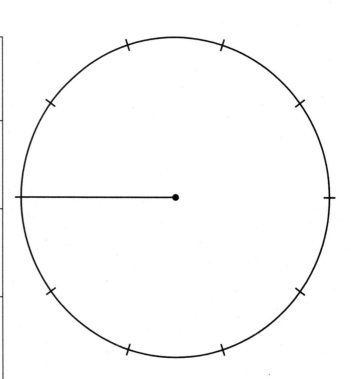

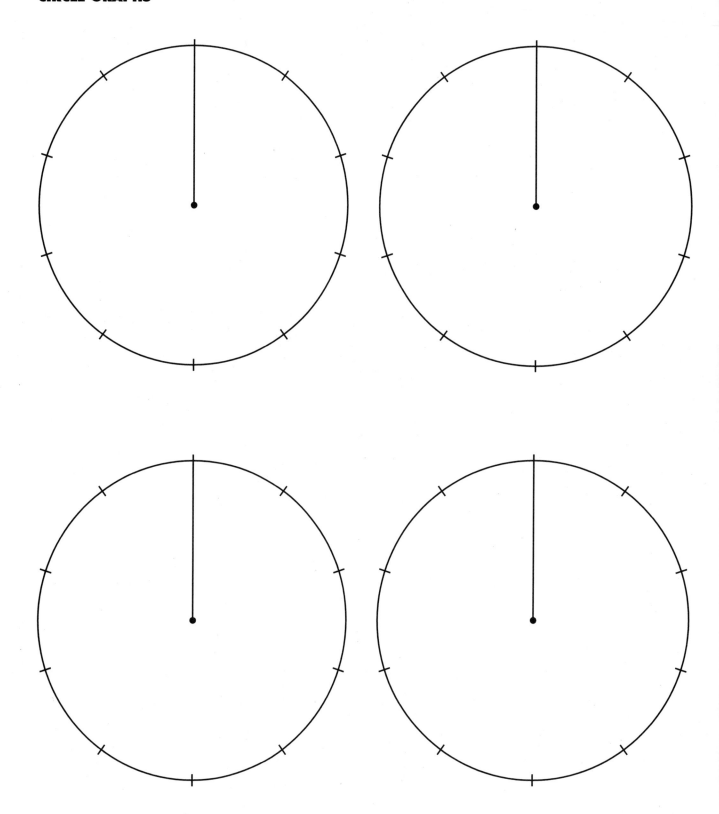

PERCENTRACTORS

Copy on transparency film. Cut out individual circles.

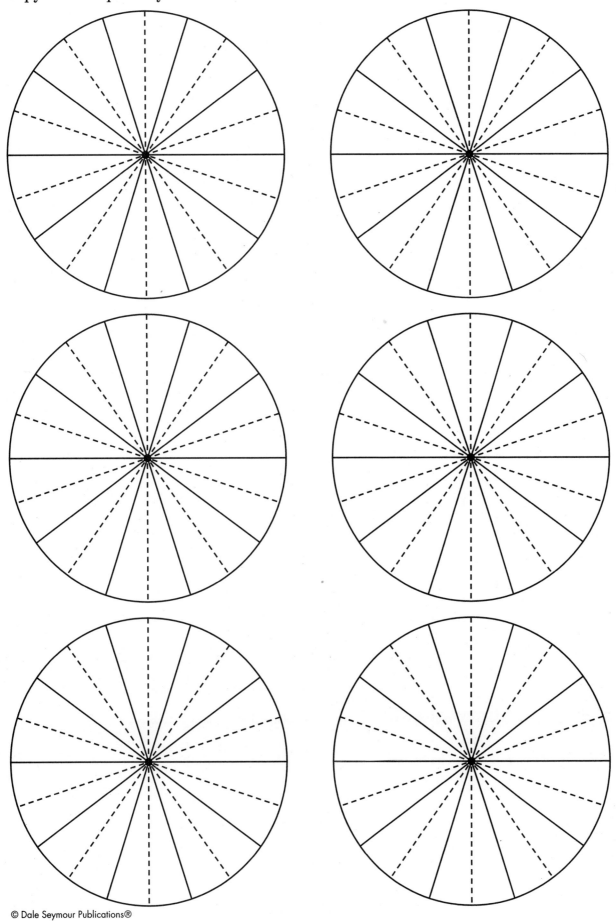

© Dale Seymour Publications®

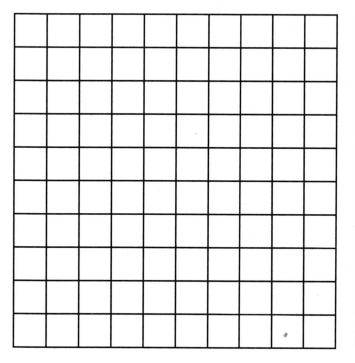

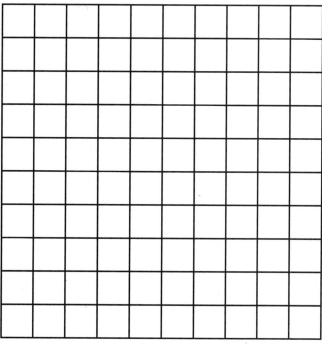

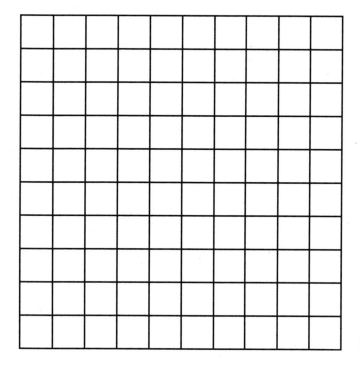

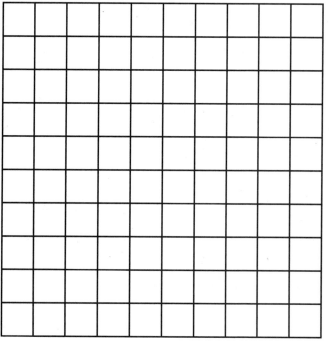

© Dale Seymour Publications®

Practice Pages

This optional section provides homework ideas for teachers who want or need to give more homework than is assigned to accompany the activities in this unit. The problems included here provide additional practice in learning about number relationships and in solving computation and number problems. For number units, you may want to use some of these if your students need more work in these areas or if you want to assign daily homework. For other units, you can use these problems so that students can continue to work on developing number and computation sense while they are focusing on other mathematical content in class. We recommend that you introduce activities in class before assigning related problems for homework.

Close to 0   This game is introduced in the unit *Mathematical Thinking at Grade 5*. If your students are familiar with the game, you can simply send home the directions, score sheet, and Numeral Cards so that students can play at home. If your students have not played the game before, introduce it in class and have students play once or twice before sending it home. Students ready for more challenge can try the variation listed at the bottom of the sheet. You might have students do this activity four times for homework in this unit.

Solving Problems in Two Ways   Students explore different ways to solve computation problems in the units *Mathematical Thinking at Grade 5* and *Building on Numbers You Know*. Here, we provide five sheets of problems that students solve in two different ways. Problems may include addition, subtraction, multiplication, or division. Students record each way they solved the problem.

Counting Puzzles   In this kind of problem, introduced in the unit *Mathematical Thinking at Grade 5*, students are given a clue about a set of numbers. Students find three numbers that match the clue (there may be many numbers that would work). If necessary, you might distribute 300 charts for students to use. Provided here are three problem sheets and one 300 chart, which you can copy for use with the problem sheets. Because this activity is included in the curriculum only as homework, it is recommended that you briefly introduce it in class before students work on it at home.

Close to 0

Materials

- One deck of Numeral Cards
- Close to 0 Score Sheet for each player

Players: 2

How to Play

1. Deal out eight Numeral Cards to each player.

2. Use any six cards to make two numbers. For example, a 6, a 5, and a 2 could make 652, 625, 526, 562, 256, or 265. Wild Cards can be used as any numeral. Try to make two numbers that, when subtracted, give you a difference that is close to 0.

3. Write these numbers and their difference on the Close to 0 Score Sheet. For example: 652 – 647 = 5. The difference is your score.

4. Put the cards you used in a discard pile. Keep the two cards you didn't use for the next round.

5. For the next round, deal six new cards to each player. Make two more numbers with a difference close to 0. When you run out of cards, mix up the discard pile and use them again.

6. After five rounds, total your scores. Lower score wins.

Variation

Deal out ten Numeral Cards to each player. Each player uses eight cards to make two numbers that, when subtracted, give a difference that is close to 0.

Close to 0 Score Sheet

Player 1   Score

Round 1:   __ __ __ – __ __ __ = _____   _____

Round 2:   __ __ __ – __ __ __ = _____   _____

Round 3:   __ __ __ – __ __ __ = _____   _____

Round 4:   __ __ __ – __ __ __ = _____   _____

Round 5:   __ __ __ – __ __ __ = _____   _____

                                              TOTAL SCORE   _____

Player 2   Score

Round 1:   __ __ __ – __ __ __ = _____   _____

Round 2:   __ __ __ – __ __ __ = _____   _____

Round 3:   __ __ __ – __ __ __ = _____   _____

Round 4:   __ __ __ – __ __ __ = _____   _____

Round 5:   __ __ __ – __ __ __ = _____   _____

                                              TOTAL SCORE   _____

0	0	1	1
0	0	1	1
2	2	3	3
2	2	3	3

4	4	5	5
4	4	5	5
<u>6</u>	<u>6</u>	7	7
<u>6</u>	<u>6</u>	7	7

Practice Page
Name That Portion

8	8	9	9
8	8	9	9
WILD CARD	WILD CARD		
WILD CARD	WILD CARD		

© Dale Seymour Publications®

184

Practice Page A

Solve this problem in two different ways, and write about
how you solved it:

   186 ÷ 6 =

Here is the first way I solved it:

Here is the second way I solved it:

Practice Page B

Solve this problem in two different ways, and write about how you solved it:

$$25 \times 12 =$$

Here is the first way I solved it:

Here is the second way I solved it:

186

Practice Page C

Solve this problem in two different ways, and write about how you solved it:

26 × 33 =

Here is the first way I solved it:

Here is the second way I solved it:

© Dale Seymour Publications®

Practice Page D

Solve this problem in two different ways, and write about how you solved it:

$$79 \div 12 =$$

Here is the first way I solved it:

Here is the second way I solved it:

Practice Page E

Solve this problem in two different ways, and write about how you solved it:

415 × 8 =

Here is the first way I solved it:

Here is the second way I solved it:

300 CHART

1	2	3	4	5	6	7	8	9	10
11	12	13	14	15	16	17	18	19	20
21	22	23	24	25	26	27	28	29	30
31	32	33	34	35	36	37	38	39	40
41	42	43	44	45	46	47	48	49	50
51	52	53	54	55	56	57	58	59	60
61	62	63	64	65	66	67	68	69	70
71	72	73	74	75	76	77	78	79	80
81	82	83	84	85	86	87	88	89	90
91	92	93	94	95	96	97	98	99	100
101	102	103	104	105	106	107	108	109	110
111	112	113	114	115	116	117	118	119	120
121	122	123	124	125	126	127	128	129	130
131	132	133	134	135	136	137	138	139	140
141	142	143	144	145	146	147	148	149	150
151	152	153	154	155	156	157	158	159	160
161	162	163	164	165	166	167	168	169	170
171	172	173	174	175	176	177	178	179	180
181	182	183	184	185	186	187	188	189	190
191	192	193	194	195	196	197	198	199	200
201	202	203	204	205	206	207	208	209	210
211	212	213	214	215	216	217	218	219	220
221	222	223	224	225	226	227	228	229	230
231	232	233	234	235	236	237	238	239	240
241	242	243	244	245	246	247	248	249	250
251	252	253	254	255	256	257	258	259	260
261	262	263	264	265	266	267	268	269	270
271	272	273	274	275	276	277	278	279	280
281	282	283	284	285	286	287	288	289	290
291	292	293	294	295	296	297	298	299	300

Practice Page F

Find three numbers that fit each clue.

1. If you count by this number, you will say 45, but you will not say 10.

2. If you count by this number, you will say 130, but you will not say 65.

3. If you count by this number, you will say 140, but you will not say 145.

Practice Page G

Find three numbers that fit each clue.

1. If you count by this number, you will say 140, but you will not say 130.

2. If you count by this number, you will say 120, but you will not say 140.

3. If you count by this number, you will say 160, but you will not say 150.

Practice Page H

Find three numbers that fit each clue.

1. If you count by this number, you will say 210, but you will
    not say 200.

2. If you count by this number, you will say 250, but you will
    not say 230.

3. If you count by this number, you will say 300, but you will
    not say 250.